CATHOLIC SOCIAL
TEACHING

CATHOLIC SOCIAL TEACHING

Revealing the Treasure

James J. Bacik

Paulist Press
New York / Mahwah, NJ

Cover image Lightspring / Shutterstock.com
Cover design by Sharyn Banks
Book design by Lynn Else

Library of Congress Cataloging-in-Publication Data
Names: Bacik, James J., 1936– author.
Title: Catholic social teaching: revealing the treasure / James J. Bacik.
Description: New York; Mahwah, NJ: Paulist Press, [2025] | Includes bibliographical references. | Summary: "This book spreads the good news of Catholic Social Teaching (CST) by commenting on its major documents and providing meditations on specific issues"—Provided by publisher.
Identifiers: LCCN 2024036539 (print) | LCCN 2024036540 (ebook) | ISBN 9780809157402 (paperback) | ISBN 9780809189083 (ebook)
Subjects: LCSH: Church and social problems—Catholic Church—History. | Social justice—Religious aspects—Catholic Church.
Classification: LCC BX1793 .B36 2025 (print) | LCC BX1793 (ebook) | DDC 261.8088/282—dc23/eng/20250110
LC record available at https://lccn.loc.gov/2024036539
LC ebook record available at https://lccn.loc.gov/2024036540

ISBN 978-0-8091-5740-2 (paperback)
ISBN 978-0-8091-8908-3 (ebook)

Published by Paulist Press
997 Macarthur Boulevard
Mahwah, NJ 07430
www.paulistpress.com

Printed and bound in the
United States of America

Dedication
For David, Martin, Christopher, and Kathryn,
who each in their own unique way
brings joy to their uncle, for which I am very grateful
to the Gracious Mystery, the Source of all blessings

CONTENTS

CONTENTS

FOREWORD

Kenneth R. Himes, OFM

What makes a good teacher? Having spent much of my life in education, as both a student and teacher, I have heard many answers to that simple question. Of course, teachers come in all shapes and sizes, diverse ages and personalities. The good ones share two loves: first, they love their subject matter, and second, they love their students. The best ones, I think, share a third characteristic: they make their students think. Yes, teachers impart information, but the best ones cause us to think and reflect on the information we are given. Truly good teachers don't tell us what to think, but encourage and show us how to think harder, and longer, and better about some matter. Good teachers are neither ideologues pushing us to adopt their viewpoint nor manipulators beguiling us into accepting some position they advocate.

A good teacher leads us into the process of learning to reflect and think for ourselves—a process that entails gathering data but also coming to understand what the data *means* and why it *matters*. Good teachers remind us that, while there may be something called artificial intelligence, there is no artificial wisdom. We only become wise by being personally reflective and acquiring insight gleaned from reasoning about our experience. Jim Bacik is a very good teacher. He invites readers to learn about the tradition of Catholic Social Teaching, but then prods us to reflect or, to use his language, meditate on the meaning and importance of that teaching material for living authentically and faithfully.

Fr. Bacik brings to the teaching task a fortunate combination of being a theologian and a pastor. Holding a doctorate in theology from Oxford University in England and having been a pastor of a vibrant campus parish in Toledo, Ohio, for three decades, Jim Bacik both knows information about Catholic Social Teaching and appreciates that many Catholics still need to learn how to integrate that element of their faith tradition with their everyday experience of life in American society.

In the first part of this slender volume, Bacik the theologian offers brief yet insightful overviews of Catholic Social Teaching. The reader gets the overall vision while the author avoids getting bogged down in scholarly details. It is the second part of the book, the longer part, where Bacik the pastor demonstrates his understanding of what he calls "the memorable first line" of Vatican II's *Pastoral Constitution on the Church in the Modern World*: "The joys and the hopes, the grief and anguish of the people of our times, especially those who are poor or afflicted are the joys and the hopes, the grief and anguish of the followers of Christ."

This is what a good pastor knows; it is what Pope Francis means when he says that Church leaders should be good shepherds who know "the smell of the sheep." The Pope has used that image several times in remarks. On one occasion in June 2021, he was speaking to a group of French priests who were doing advanced theological studies in Rome. He reminded them that they should not go into the field to apply theories without considering the environment in which they will be working or the people entrusted to their care. "I wish you to be shepherds with 'the smell of the sheep.'" Francis wanted these young priests to realize that pastors should be "people capable of living, of laughing and crying with your people, in a word, of communicating with them." With characteristic bluntness, he told them that a priesthood isolated from the people of God is neither a Catholic priesthood nor a Christian one.

Jim Bacik knows both his theological material and his flock. He has not simply written a book about Catholic Social Teaching; he has written a book that urges readers to reflect for themselves upon that tradition and to do so in the pastoral settings in which they live and work as American Catholics. The theologian and the pastor have both been at work in crafting this brief yet rewarding book.

ACKNOWLEDGMENTS

When writing this book, various voices played in my mind. There was the late scripture scholar Fr. Eugene Maly urging me to embrace and apply without fear the findings of modern biblical scholarship; Karl Rahner, one of the most influential theologians in the history of the Church, assuring me that the Catholic theological tradition has relevance in the modern world; my good friend Richard Gaillardetz, who died too soon, giving me welcome advice on complex theological issues; my Paulist editor, Paul McMahon, who provided helpful changes and additions to the text; my longtime friend, social activist, and professor of English, Patricia Schnapp, RSM, who, five decades ago, encouraged me to write monthly articles of reflection and has supported all my writings, including proofreading almost all my books; my friend Pam Meseroll, who helped organize my notes, files, and drafts; my sister Barbara Bacik Tyrrel, who encouraged me by word and example to be more attentive to the voice of the Holy Spirit; and finally, my sister Patricia Bacik Safford, my typist and proofreader, who identified offensive, arcane, and inappropriate language that needed rewriting. I am grateful for all the voices that inspired this book.

INTRODUCTION

The title of this book, *Catholic Social Teaching: Revealing the Treasure*, is reminiscent of an earlier 1984 book published by the Center for Social Concerns on Catholic Social Teaching (CST). It was called, appropriately, *Catholic Social Teaching*, with the catchy subtitle, *Our Best Kept Secret*. Since then, many fine books have been published about CST helping to spread the good news of this valuable tradition. Unfortunately, however, recent surveys show that most Catholics still have very little knowledge of this treasure. My hope is that this book will contribute to the ongoing effort to spread the message of CST to a larger audience. To realize this hope, we will examine Catholic Social Teaching in various contexts—historical, pastoral, theological, political, and spiritual—designed to reveal more of the wisdom, power, and relevance of this rich resource.

This book is divided into two major parts. The first part deals with a selected list of significant Catholic Social Teaching documents. In chapter 1, we examine the historical contexts of some of the important papal and conciliar documents, understanding them not as abstract, detached doctrine but as part of a story that has interesting characters, serious conflicts, and hidden meanings. For example, it is instructive to realize that American Catholic workers and their dedicated pastors played a vital role in persuading Pope Leo to support labor unions in his encyclical *Rerum novarum*. It is revealing to know that Pope John Paul II's encyclical *Centesimus annus* produced sharply polarized responses from conservative and liberal American Catholics. And it is encouraging to recall the positive impact that Pope Francis's encyclical *Laudato si'* had on the success of the Paris Agreement on global warming.

In the second chapter, we examine the pastoral context through the seven themes of Catholic Social Teaching. For example, preaching on the preferential option for the poor is more effective if it avoids inflicting a false sense of guilt on affluent parishioners, encouraging them rather to help empower poor persons to take charge of their own lives. Approaching the first theme, "Life and Dignity of the Human Person," concretely in the context of liberation theology reveals the power of social sin to oppress marginalized groups and create societal inequities. My commentaries on these seven themes also include a political context drawn from the outstanding book, *Toward a Politics of Communion*, by the highly respected British theologian Anna Rowlands. Making her work better known to our American audience is an important contribution of this book.

Chapter 3 treats the pastoral letters of the U.S. Conference of Catholic Bishops within the cultural and societal trends that have affected the reception of these documents. This analysis reveals the sharp divide within the Catholic community between "traditional" members and "progressives," a split intensified by the growing influence of partisan politics. In this chapter, we also consider the unique pastoral letter, *Empowered by the Spirit: Campus Ministry Faces the Future*. This letter has never been included in a public list of CST documents before, even though, I contend, it has done more to spread CST than any other pastoral letter, a significant claim that I support in this chapter.

The meditations in the second part of the book are most effective when seen in a spiritual context that reflects real life concerns. For example, volunteer workers who wonder if their charitable work is worthwhile can be encouraged in their faith conviction that all good work participates in God's ongoing creation of a more just world. The issues in part two—including the morality of abortion, overcoming racism, and caring for creation—are complex and need to be approached from multiple perspectives. Typically, the meditations include relevant background material and questions to guide reflection as they relate to CST principles. In some cases, suggestions for concrete actions in applying CST teaching have been included.

Hopefully, this book, with its distinctive contexts and features, will indeed reveal and disseminate more of our rich resource of Catholic Social Teaching for promoting the common good.

ABBREVIATIONS

CA   *Centesimus annus* (1991)
CCC   *Catechism of the Catholic Church* (1993)
CP   *The Challenge of Peace* (1983)
CSDC   *Compendium of the Social Doctrine of the Church*
        (2004)
CV   *Caritas in veritate* (2009)
DCE   *Deus caritas est* (2005)
EJ   *Economic Justice for All* (1986)
ES   *Empowered by the Spirit* (1985)
FT   *Fratelli tutti* (2020)
GS   *Gaudium et spes* (1965)
JM   *Justitia in mundo* (1971)
LE   *Laborem exercens* (1981)
LS   *Laudato si'* (2015)
MM   *Mater et magistra* (1961)
OA   *Octogesima adveniens* (1971)
PP   *Populorum progressio* (1967)
PT   *Pacem in terris* (1963)
QA   *Quadragesimo anno* (1931)
RN   *Rerum novarum* (1891)
SRS   *Sollicitudo rei socialis* (1987)

Part I
THE DOCUMENTS

1

PAPAL AND CONCILIAR DOCUMENTS

Catholic Social Teaching (CST), a rich resource for dealing with the complex problems that threaten the well-being of the human family, deserves to be better known and applied. Modern CST is presented in major papal and conciliar documents, ranging from Pope Leo XIII's groundbreaking 1891 encyclical, *Rerum novarum*, which began the tradition, to the most recent encyclical, *Fratelli tutti*, issued by Pope Francis in 2020. There is no official listing of CST documents, but theologians generally agree on which encyclicals and documents from Vatican II belong on the list.

Catholic Social Teaching is an evolving dynamic tradition best understood in historical and theological contexts, including the leaders and movements that set the stage for the official teaching. The context also includes what theologians call "reception" analysis, which examines how various Catholic leaders and groups have received the official documents.

The Catholic moral theologian Charles Curran has identified important continuities in Catholic Social Teaching.[1] CST has developed organically with subsequent documents building on previous ones, starting with *Rerum novarum*, and has consistently based its major provisions on the dignity of the human person known by reason and revelation. It has regularly promoted the "common good" that enables individuals and communities to achieve their own fulfillment. Its teaching on the proper role of the state has grounded a consistent critique of both liberal individualism and socialist collectivism.

Curran has also noted serious tensions, limitations, and discontinuities in the CST tradition. After Vatican II, the official teaching made greater use of explicit Christian resources to ground its provisions. It also widened its audience to include not only Catholics but all people of good will, without, however, developing a coherent method for reaching both audiences. The tradition has not done well in relating its moral teaching to the liturgy, the font and summit of Christian life. Nor has it given enough attention to the vocation of all baptized persons to strive for holiness and spread the kingdom in the world. Finally, Curran insists that there have been clear reversals in CST. For example, Vatican II affirmed religious liberty as a fundamental human right, an evident radical departure from previous teaching.

Rerum novarum (*On the Condition of Labor*)

On May 15, 1891, Pope Leo XIII (1810–1903), issued the landmark encyclical *Rerum novarum*. This historic document, urged and supported by bishops in the United States, brought the Catholic Church out of a reactionary era into a period of constructive dialogue with the modern world. The social doctrine of this encyclical, which recognized the rights of workers to organize in response to the abuses of unbridled capitalism, was very moderate in comparison to some of the political movements of the time and appears almost commonplace from our perspective today. However, it is historically important because it reversed a long-standing church policy of intransigent opposition to all aspects of the modern world and inaugurated a new period in which Catholicism has become an important partner in the continuing dialogue on how best to organize human affairs politically and economically.

The French Revolution of 1789 produced an intense defensive reaction among Catholic leaders because they feared that the call for liberty and equality would lead to extensive defections from the Church. This negative reaction was epitomized by the *Syllabus of Errors*, promulgated by Pope Pius IX in 1864 denouncing the entire modern project, including democracy, individual rights, and religious liberty. This intransigent position seemed to relegate the Catholic Church to the status of a sect existing on the margins of the modern world without any effective means of influencing contemporary developments.

Less than thirty years later, Pope Leo XIII changed the tenor of the relationship between the Church and modernity by replacing blanket condemnations with constructive discussions about how the Church and state could collaborate for the common good.

Typical of CST documents, *Rerum novarum* was influenced by prior movements, including developments in Europe and the United States.[2] Professor Marvin Mich begins his portrayal of the preparation for RN in the year 1848, when Europe experienced a series of protests in major cities against the social and economic devastation caused by the Industrial Revolution. That year, a German priest, Wilhelm Emmanuel von Ketteler, preached six powerful sermons on "the social question," the poverty and sufferings of the German working class that touched the conscience of the nation and spawned an international movement known as "Social Catholicism." The movement was aided by the Fribourg Union, a think tank of concerned laity and clergy that applied Catholic moral principles to creating a more just social order. It offered some specific remedies: for example, prohibiting child labor in factories; limiting working hours for factory workers; closing unsanitary workshops; allowing Sunday rest; separating the sexes in the workshops; and caring for injured workers.

Mich makes a strong case that "Social Catholicism and the Fribourg Union had a direct influence on Pope Leo," who was regularly briefed on their yearly meetings and met personally with some of their leaders.[3] The movement considered the publication of RN to be a confirmation of their positions and a completion of their mission.

In this historic encyclical, Pope Leo XIII strongly attacked socialist proposals to transfer property from private individuals to the state as ineffective, unjust, and harmful to workers. To build social harmony, the pope insisted that workers have the duties to perform their agreed-upon tasks and to refrain from violence, rioting, and insurrection. Likewise, employers have the duties to respect the dignity of workers and provide suitable work for them. In a move that helped the U.S. Church maintain the allegiance of working-class Catholics, the pope affirmed the right of workers to form unions, while also warning against power-hungry leaders.

The American Catholic Church also had an important role in shaping the focus and tone of RN.[4] In the late nineteenth century, a strong labor movement arose in the United States to assist workers suffering from the ill effects of the Industrial Revolution. The Knights of Labor, founded in 1868, successfully managed several large strikes that gained popular support and, by 1886, had a membership of 700,000, including many Catholics and a Catholic union leader, Terrence Powderly. At the peak of its power, a Canadian bishop condemned the union and forbade Catholics to join it. In the United States, the Knights enjoyed the support of many parish priests as well as most U.S. bishops, who voted ten to two against condemning the union. In 1887, Archbishop James Gibbons, who was going to Rome to be installed as a cardinal, took with him a long letter authored primarily by Archbishop John Ireland of St. Paul, Minnesota. The letter defended the Knights of Labor and urged Pope Leo XIII not to condemn it, arguing that the American Church was still perceived as "the Friend of the People," and that a condemnation would lose the working class for generations to come. Marvin Mich claims that the success of the American Church in maintaining the loyalty of the working class was a "major influence" on Leo XIII's decision to write the encyclical.[5]

Gaudium et spes (Pastoral Constitution on the Church in the Modern World)

In important ways, *Gaudium et spes* is the most authoritative and significant document of modern Catholic Social Teaching. It is the fruit of a long process during the Second Vatican Council (1962–1965) that involved episcopal initiatives, theological consultations, multiple drafts, and a final affirmative vote of 2,309 to 75 and promulgation on December 7, 1965, the last day of the Council.

The constitution is not just of historical interest but maintains vital contemporary significance as the Church today, under Pope Francis, struggles to appropriate the teachings and spirit of Vatican II. The pope frequently references *Gaudium et spes* when he is urging Catholics to move out of the sanctuary and establish field hospitals in the world.

The seventy draft documents prepared for discussion at Vatican II all dealt primarily with internal Church issues, such as liturgy, the role of the laity, and priestly formation. During the first session of the Council, influential leaders spoke in favor of a separate document to address the external mission of the Church to share in Christ's mission to transform the world. Brazilian Auxiliary Bishop Hélder Câmara joined with Belgian

Cardinal Leo Suenens to push for more attention to the problems of the poor in developing countries. Cardinal Montini, who soon became Pope Paul VI, gave a speech calling the Council to address the Church's role in society. These interventions initiated a long process of drafting a document that included input from theologians Bernard Haring and Henri de Lubac, advice from fourteen lay persons, and hundreds of amendments from the bishops. The final version of the pastoral constitution included compromises that ensured its passage.

The memorable first line of *Gaudium et spes* set the tone and theme of the whole document: "The joys and the hopes, the griefs and the anxieties of the [people] of this age, especially those who are poor or in any way afflicted, these are the joys and hopes, the griefs and anxieties of the followers of Christ" (no. 1).

The pastoral constitution repeatedly insists that Christians must be involved in the task of transforming the world. We are to follow Christ, who came as a servant so that "this world might be fashioned anew according to God's design and reach its fulfillment" (no. 2). Since human society should be renewed, the Church must scrutinize the signs of the times, make the concerns of society its own, and bring the light of the Gospel to bear on all aspects of human existence in the world (cf. no. 3). The bishops at the council were convinced that the church could make important contributions to improving the social order, so that it will be "founded on truth, built on justice, and animated by love," moving gradually toward "a more humane balance" (no. 26).

The constitution goes on to exhort Christians to strive to discharge their earthly duties conscientiously and in the spirit of the gospel. The bishops attacked the view that religion consists of acts of worship alone, insisting that "this split between the faith which many profess and their daily lives deserves to be counted among the more serious errors of our age" (no. 43). No one should be content with "a merely individualistic morality" because the "obligations of justice and love are fulfilled only if each person also promotes and assists the public and private institutions dedicated to bettering the conditions of human life" (no. 30).

The council rooted its call for Christian involvement in transforming the world in a solid understanding of human existence. As a unique individual created in the image of God, each human being possesses an intrinsic value and essential dignity which calls for absolute respect. At the same time, we are social creatures who live in an increasingly interdependent world. "The progress of the human person and the advance of society itself hinge on each other" (no. 25). Social institutions should have the welfare of persons as their primary goal. Imbalances and tensions in the economic, political, and social order impede human progress and development.

As social creatures, we have important rights: to choose a state of life, to found a family, to receive an education, to have gainful employment, and to enjoy religious liberty. Respect for persons demands that we reject whatever is opposed to life itself, such as murder, genocide, abortion, and euthanasia; whatever violates the integrity of individuals, such as torture and coercion; and whatever insults human dignity, such as subhuman living conditions and disgraceful working conditions. This respect should be extended to those who think or act differently, as well as to enemies who stand with us before God, the sole searcher of hearts. Every kind of discrimination based on sex, race, color, social conditions, languages, or religion must be eradicated. Furthermore, we need healthy human institutions to safeguard the rights and dignity of all people (cf. no. 29).

In responding to contemporary social concerns, *Gaudium et spes* insists that the Church as a whole as well as individual Christians should function as servants and follow the path of dialogue. The Church must neither withdraw into a ghetto nor attempt to reestablish Christendom. Christians do not have a blueprint for social progress, nor are they tied to any particular political party or economic system. The proper Christian concern is for the kingdom of God, but the divine reign touches all dimensions of human existence, including the social and institutional. Christ gave the Church a religious mission, but fidelity to this task can help transform and renew society. Thus, the Church enters the public realm as a dialogue partner, bringing the light of the gospel to bear on contemporary questions and seeking collaboration with all people of good will. At the same time, Christians expect to learn from the genuine progress made in society and from the authentic insights generated by the culture.

In conclusion, the bishops repeated that their proposals are intended to help all people, whether believers in God or not, to a "keener awareness of their own destiny, to make the world conform better to the surpassing dignity of man, to strive for a more deeply rooted sense of universal brotherhood, and to meet the pressing appeals of our time with a generous and common effort of love" (no. 91).

Examining *Gaudium et spes* six decades after its publication, some of its limitations are more evident. It is, for example, overly optimistic in its assessment of the modern world, failing to put enough emphasis on the destructive contradictions in contemporary society such as nationalism, racism, hedonism, and sexism. Liberation theology in its many forms has uncovered new biblical and theological justifications and motivations for Christian involvement in the struggle against injustice. Social scientists have given us a more nuanced view of the positive role of institutions, as well as their oppressive tendencies. The media, which shrinks the earth to a global village, has made us more aware of the destructive consequences of social sin.

Despite its limitations, the pastoral constitution challenges every effort to reduce Christianity to personal religious experience and private morality. The document provides a solid explanation of why Christians must be concerned with institutional life and public policy questions. It encourages dialogue with the social sciences in reading the signs of the times and reminds us that CST is a rich resource for meeting the contemporary threats to our culture and society. Finally, *Gaudium et spes* encourages us to continue the process of appropriating the teachings and spirit of the Second Vatican Council.

Centesimus annus (*The Hundredth Year*)

Pope John Paul II published this lengthy encyclical of 114 pages on May 1, 1991. It is of special interest because of the way it was received in the United States.

The initial reaction to the encyclical focused primarily on one topic—the pope's position on capitalism. Neoconservatives exulted in the positive statements made by the pope about a free market economy. For example, Richard Neuhaus, editor of *First Things* and a 1990 convert to Catholicism, wrote an article in the *Wall Street Journal* the day after the encyclical was published claiming that it was a "ringing endorsement of the market economy." Obviously Neuhaus had an advance copy and presumably rushed a response to influence public perception of the document. Correctly noting the great emphasis the pope put on a Christian understanding of human nature, but going far beyond any explicit statements in the encyclical, Neuhaus concluded that "capitalism is the economic corollary of the Christian understanding of man's nature and destiny." He went on to say that the pope's teaching means interpretations of Catholic Social Teaching along socialist or semi-socialist lines are in serious error. Furthermore, he suggested that the "controlling assumptions of the American bishops' 1986 pastoral letter, 'Economic Justice for All' must now be recognized as unrepresentative of the church's authoritative teaching."[6]

Taking a more moderate position, the neoconservative author Michael Novak lauded the encyclical for bringing "the American understanding of economic liberty into the Catholic tradition."[7] In the past, Novak had criticized papal teaching for failing to appreciate the true genius of the American capitalist system. According to Novak, Pope Paul VI was overly critical of capitalism because he failed to understand the way the free market produces wealth through the encouragement of initiative, creativity, and hard work. He found the same fundamental problem in John Paul II's 1981 encyclical, *Laborem exercens*, which misunderstood capitalism as actually practiced in the United States, failing to see how it serves the common good by promoting investment and growth and by enabling workers to achieve a better life.

In *Centesimus annus*, however, Novak found quotes that sounded more like what he wrote in his book, *The Spirit of Democratic Capitalism*. His prime example was this lengthy passage:

> It is disciplined work in close collaboration with others that makes possible the creation of evermore extensive working communities which can be relied upon to transform man's natural and human environments. Important virtues are involved in this process such as diligence, industriousness, prudence in undertaking reasonable risks, reliability and fidelity in interpersonal relationships as well as courage in carrying out decisions which are difficult and painful but necessary both for the overall working of a business and in meeting possible setbacks. (no. 32)

Liberal commentators, though, insisted that the neoconservatives were guilty of a one-sided reading of the encyclical when they failed to note what the pope said about the limits and problems connected with the free market. For instance, John Coleman, SJ, an expert on religion and society, insisted that "anyone who reads this encyclical and says that this is an endorsement of the functioning system of capitalism as it exists in the U.S. is an ideologue."[8] Liberals also found material in the encyclical to support this point. For instance, the pope wrote that "a business cannot be considered only as a 'society of capital goods'; it is also a 'society of persons' in which people participate in different ways and with specific responsibilities, whether they supply the necessary capital for the company's activities or take part in such activities through their labour" (no. 43). Since "economic freedom is only one element of human freedom… there are qualitative needs which cannot be satisfied by market mechanisms" and "important human needs which escape its logic" (nos. 39, 40). The pope also warned against an "idolatry of the market" and the cultivation of a "consumerist mentality" in which people are "ensnared in the web of false and superficial gratifications" (no. 41).

The sharp division among American Catholics over free market economics has only intensified during the last three decades due to the growing influence of partisan politics. We can hope that the broad perspectives of Catholic Social Teaching on economic matters will eventually encourage constructive dialogue between American conservatives and liberals.

Caritas in veritate
(Charity in Truth)

This 2009 encyclical is of special importance because it deals with our ecological crisis. Early in his papacy, Benedict XVI periodically made statements encouraging responsible stewardship of the earth. In this encyclical, he devoted a whole section to the environment, offering some important theological perspectives. "The environment is God's gift to everyone, and in our use of it we have a responsibility toward the poor, toward future generations and toward humanity as a whole" (no. 48). He rejected extreme attitudes toward nature: a "new pantheism" that makes nature more important than the human person, and a "total technical dominion over nature" that leads to "reckless exploitation." On the contrary, Christians see nature as "a wondrous work of the Creator containing a grammar that sets forth ends and criteria for its wise use" (no. 48).

Considering the "energy problem," Benedict reminded the highly industrialized countries that they have a moral obligation to avoid hoarding and exploiting nonrenewable resources (cf. no. 49). They "can and must lower their domestic energy consumption" through the use of alternative forms of energy and through a "greater ecological sensibility" among ordinary citizens that challenges a hedonistic and consumerist lifestyle, while promoting human solidarity and the common good (no. 51). Benedict insisted that "the overall moral tenor of society" is decisive in dealing with the environmental crisis. We need a "human ecology" that respects life in all stages of development as a solid basis for an "environmental ecology" that treasures nature as a gift from God (no. 51).

Pope Benedict elaborated on these perspectives in his 2010 World Day of Peace message, with the subtitle, "If You Want to Cultivate Peace, Protect Creation." Integral human development is threatened not only by wars and terrorism, but also by threats arising from the neglect and misuse of the earth. Once again, acknowledging our growing ecological crisis, Benedict cited a long list of problems, starting with climate change and including pollution of rivers and aquifers, the loss of biodiversity, deforestation of tropical regions, the plight of environmental refugees, and unequal access to natural resources. In response to this crisis, we need "a profound cultural renewal," including "a lifestyle marked by sobriety and solidarity" (no. 5). In the past, some academic critics have claimed that the biblical injunction giving human beings dominion over the earth (Gen 1:28) has contributed to our environmental problems. Responding to this criticism, the pope insisted that God's command calls us to renounce selfish exploitation of the earth and to assume responsible stewardship of the natural world (cf. no. 6).

Benedict grounds concern for the environment in a "broad global vision of the world; a responsible common effort to move beyond approaches based on selfish, nationalistic interests toward a vision constantly open to the needs of the people. We cannot remain indifferent to what is happening around us, for the deterioration of any one part of the planet affects us all" (no. 11). This global perspective challenges us "to examine our lifestyles and the prevailing models of consumption and production which are often unsustainable from a social, environmental and even economic point of view" (no. 11). It also calls for citizens of the industrialized countries to develop a deeper sense of solidarity with the poor around the world and with future generations. This new "global solidarity" demands a more equitable distribution of natural resources and the development of alternative sources of energy, especially "the immense potential of solar energy" (no. 10).

Pope Benedict also proposed some important components of a contemporary ecospirituality. Many individuals "experience peace and tranquility, renewal and reinvigoration when they come into close contact with the beauty and harmony of nature....As we care for creation we realize that God, through creation cares for us" (no. 13). As Christians, we contemplate the earth in the light of the redeeming work of Christ, who sent the Spirit to guide the course of history until that day when he will return in glory and there will be "new heavens and a new earth" (no. 14). For Benedict, a comprehensive ecospirituality combines care for the earth and a passion for justice and peace in the world. "If you want to cultivate peace, protect creation" (no. 14).

Deus caritas est (God Is Love)

Pope Benedict published this encyclical in 2009, during the worldwide financial crisis. It is long and it draws on the traditional (most of the 159 endnotes cite previous social encyclicals), wide-ranging (topics include globalization, climate change, and food shortages), and theologically sophisticated (the product of one of the finest theological minds ever to serve as Bishop of Rome). It is of special interest because of the various responses this encyclical elicited. For example, German Chancellor Angela Merkel, a Lutheran, was impressed with Benedict's consistent anthropology that places the human person at the center of "the responsible politics" needed, especially during the economic crisis. She was especially taken with his statement, "The primary capital to be safeguarded and valued is man, the human person in his or her integrity" (no. 25).

Indeed, Benedict grounded his many recommendations in a consistent Christian humanism. For him, all human beings "feel the interior impulse to love authentically." The search for love and truth is a "vocation planted by God in the heart and mind of every human person" (no. 1). This search is purified and liberated by Jesus Christ, who loves us and is concerned with our personal development. Our common vocation to promote integral human development calls for a free assumption of responsibility in solidarity with others. A "transcendent vision of the person" recognizes the need for God who enables us to avoid the trap of self-sufficiency that leads to a distorted form of development. To achieve authentic human development, we need a new "transcendent humanism" that embraces "the duties of solidarity," often neglected in our globalized world that "makes us neighbors but does not make us brothers" (no. 11). God's free gift of love calls into being the human race, a fraternal communion transcending every barrier. We grow in maturity not by isolating ourselves, but by placing ourselves in relation with God and other persons. Reason guided by faith recognizes that the unity of the human family does not submerge the identity of individual persons and cultures, but makes them more open to others and unites them more closely in their legitimate diversity. As Angela Merkel and others recognized, Pope Benedict's anthropology, with its strong sense of communion and solidarity, provides a solid basis for his concrete proposals designed to promote the common good.

In response to *Deus caritas est*, the *Wall Street Journal* published an article that highlighted Benedict's call for "a true world political authority," one with "real teeth" that would exercise greater oversight of the world's financial markets.[9] This authority would be responsible for avoiding international financial catastrophes. A Vatican advisor suggested that the United Nations could establish a "Socioeconomic Security Council"—similar to the current Security Council dedicated to preserving the peace—that could help avoid global financial disasters. He said that Benedict was not proposing "a kind of superstate" but "an internationally recognized institution" that could intervene in crisis situations.

The pope's innovative proposal met with serious opposition from critics in the United States, who considered it to be naive and an unwarranted intrusion on national sovereignty. Anticipating such objections, Benedict invited his readers to move beyond a narrow nationalism and seek the common good that promotes authentic integral human development inspired by the values of charity in truth. He recognized that such an international authority needs the power to ensure compliance with its decisions in order to promote a just and peaceful international order. In response to his critics, Benedict also employed the traditional CST principle of subsidiarity, which insists that local issues be managed by local authorities if possible and that higher levels of government should intervene to protect human rights and serve the common good only when these goals cannot be achieved at the lower level. In other words, the UN could intervene in economic affairs only if nation states could not avoid an international financial crisis on their own.

Laudato si' (On Care for Our Common Home)

This encyclical is of special interest for various reasons: it deals with a matter of supreme importance—preserving our planet; it provides a good example of how the CST documents build on secular movements; and it is a great example of promoting the reception of encyclical teaching. In 1962, Rachel Carson published *Silent Spring*, which documented the environmental harm caused by indiscriminate use of pesticides. The book energized the U.S. environmental movement and led to the creation of the Environmental Protection Agency (EPA) in 1970. At the same time, the movement received a major boost with the celebration of the first Earth Day on April 22, 1970, which drew an estimated twenty million people to rallies around the country. The leaders wanted "to shake up the political establishment and force this issue onto the national agenda."[10] That first Earth Day succeeded in bringing together individuals and groups concerned about various types of environmental degradation, including oil spills, factory pollution, toxic dumps, and wildlife extinction.

Since then, the environmental movement has found inspiration in individual heroes, such as Chico Mendes, a Brazilian rubber tapper who became an environmental activist. Energized and guided by his participation in a Catholic base community, he founded a national union of rubber tappers and fought to stop the destruction of the Amazon rainforest to clear land for cattle ranching. His activism, which included direct physical confrontations with forest-clearing groups, cost him his life, as ranchers shot him in his home in front of his family on December 22, 1988, just one week after his forty-fourth birthday. Inspired by the gospel, Chico Mendes developed an expanded vision of his social action: "At first I thought I was fighting to save rubber trees, then I thought I was fighting to save the Amazon rainforest. Now I realize I am fighting for humanity."[11]

After the death of Chico Mendes, many more innocent persons were killed in land conflicts in the Amazon Basin. Prominent among the activist victims was Dorothy Stang, a Notre Dame de Namur sister, who was born in Dayton, Ohio, and became a naturalized Brazilian citizen. She worked diligently for three decades defending the land rights of peasants who extracted products from the Amazon rainforest and were often harassed by criminal gangs employed by ranchers determined to turn the forest into grazing land for cattle. On February 12, 2005, Sr. Dorothy was on her way to a meeting when two men approached her and shot her repeatedly at close range. On April 12, 2010, a rancher was finally convicted by a Brazilian court of ordering her murder and was sentenced to thirty years in prison. Sr. Dorothy's life story has been portrayed in a documentary film, *The Killing of Sister Dorothy* (narrated by Martin Sheen), and in the opera *Angel of the Amazon*, which depicts the events leading to her martyrdom. Like Chico Mendes, Sr. Dorothy Stang became a folk hero and martyr for the environmental cause.

In 1990, the twentieth annual Earth Day went global, attracting an estimated 200 million people to rallies in 141 countries. These worldwide demonstrations stressed the importance of protecting the environment through recycling and set the stage for the United Nations Earth Summit, held in Rio de Janeiro in 1992. For Earth Day 2000, the organizers made use of the Internet to connect approximately five thousand grassroots environmental groups from 184 countries around the world in a massive effort to raise consciousness on the problem of global warming and the importance of developing clean energy.

In the twenty-first century, much environmental activism has centered on the problem of global warming. During the United Nations Climate Change Conference, held in Copenhagen in December of 2009, about 50,000 activists gathered nearby for a People's Climate Summit that called for radical systematic changes to control global warming and urged world leaders to reach a binding agreement on carbon emissions.

Internationally, committed individuals and groups have adopted simple practices to combat global warming: for example, recycling, walking or biking to work, eating less meat, driving more fuel-efficient cars, and installing compact fluorescent light bulbs. A growing number of Catholics have taken the St. Francis Pledge to Care for Creation and the Poor, promising prayer, study, assessment, action, and advocacy to combat global warming. At the grassroots level, environmental issues continue to generate significant interest and activity.

The environmental movement found an ally in Pope Benedict XVI, the "Green Pope," who recognized the dangers of ecological degradation and affirmed practical efforts to protect the planet. At the same time, the pope proposed theological perspectives that challenged some extremes in the movement and provided helpful guidance for the common task of caring for the earth.

In his 2015 encyclical, *Laudato si'*, Pope Francis builds on the good work of the environmental movement and his predecessor, Pope Benedict. In chapter 1 of the encyclical, Francis raises up St. Francis of Assisi as an outstanding example of care for both the poor and the earth, and insists on the "immediacy and urgency" of the ecological crisis. Based on scientific studies, he insists that global warming is "a result of human activity" (no. 23) and notes that the environment is "defenseless before the interests of a deified market, which becomes the only rule" (no. 56).

In the second chapter, Francis speaks poetically about creation. For example, God calls us to "till and keep the garden of the world," which is "a caress of God" and a "precious book" of the "exhaustible riches of God" (nos. 30–48). Chapter 3 analyzes the role of technology, recognizing its accomplishments in improving human life, but warning of its "ironclad logic" to gain "lordship over all." An authentic ecospirituality does not seek to dominate the earth but aspires to a "responsible stewardship" of the earth. Since "everything is interrelated," we must join care for the earth with care for all human beings, including the unborn and the poor (nos. 49–66). In chapter 4, Francis calls for an "integral ecology" that provides human beings with "a secure living space," including livable cities, adequate housing, and good public transportation. We must protect indigenous cultures and hand on to the next generation a "habitable planet" (nos. 67–71). Chapter 5 urges international cooperation to protect the environment and suggests that the Church has a role to play by promoting dialogue and providing a spiritual perspective.

The final chapter of *Laudato si'* is a rich resource for cultivating a Christian ecospirituality. To counter consumerism, we need to adopt a simpler lifestyle: for example, using less water, cooking only what is needed, and carpooling. We need to develop "ecological virtues," solid habits formed by a healthy family life and nourished by the Church that incline us to combine care for the earth and love for the most vulnerable. Pope Francis concludes his beautifully written, faith-inspired encyclical with a prayer asking the "Lord of life" to help us "protect all life" and prepare for the kingdom of "justice, peace, love and beauty."

Since the publication of *Laudato si'* in May 2015, our common home has experienced many serious disasters. For example, the Australian bush fires that burned from June 2019 to March 2020 decimated some 72,000 square miles, destroyed almost 6,000 buildings, and took the lives of more than 450 persons. They also killed an estimated one billion animals—an astounding number attested by competent experts— and sent polluted air almost 7,000 miles across the South Pacific Ocean to Chile and Argentina.

In 2018, there were at least five major natural disasters in the United States. Early in the year, mudslides in Montecito, California, flattened homes, covered freeways, and killed twenty-one people. In the spring, flash floods devastated Ellicott City, Maryland, causing millions of dollars of damage to buildings and sweeping away to his death an Air Force veteran, Eddison Hermund, who tried to help others. In September, Hurricane Florence hit the Carolinas, destroying many homes and directly causing the death of twenty-four people. Just a few months later, Hurricane Michael left a trail of destruction across Florida, Georgia, and the Carolinas, destroying many cities, including Panama City, Florida, and taking more than fifty lives. Near the end of 2018, wildfires swept through northern California, killing eighty-five people, the deadliest fire in the history of the Golden State. During 2021, extreme weather events in the United States caused at least 688 direct or indirect fatalities. In August 2023, wildfires swept through the Hawaiian island of Maui, wiping out the town of Lahaina and killing an estimated ninety-seven people. The dire warnings in *Laudato Si'* of imminent disasters have proved to be all too accurate.

Pope Francis explicitly intended his encyclical to support the proposed Paris Climate Agreement, which was later adopted by a consensus of 195 countries and officially signed on April 22, 2016. All countries agreed to make progress reducing greenhouse gas emissions, with each nation free to set their own specific goals and timing. It is difficult to verify compliance, but experts generally agree that governments must do much more and act more quickly to avoid impending disasters.

Since the publication of *Laudato si'* in 2015, there have been many efforts to put its suggestions into practice. For example, on the fourth anniversary of its publication, the Catholic Climate Covenant cosponsored a major conference at Creighton University in Omaha, Nebraska, attended by two hundred invited guests, including scholars and activists from around the country, three bishops, and a Vatican representative. Participants shared success stories: universities reducing their carbon footprint; hospitals eliminating the use of bottled water; parishes using more solar energy; Catholic institutions divesting stocks in fossil fuel companies; pastors giving greater attention in their homilies to caring for the earth and the poor; and parishioners supporting political candidates committed to dealing with the ecological crisis and backing legislation that protects the environment.

Then-Bishop Robert McElroy of San Diego, who gave the keynote address,[12] urged parishes and schools to become "centers of truth-telling" that challenge those "industries and economic interests that despoil our planet." He also recognized young people as "the prophetic voice of environmental justice in our nation," who have the power to open the minds of their elders to the threat that climate change poses on future generations.

Although *Laudato si'* has important things to say about the environmental crisis, including the claim that there is a scientific consensus on human responsibility for global warming, the encyclical has a broader purpose and more comprehensive focus, which is developed under the heading of an "integral ecology" based on a solid anthropology. According to Pope Francis, the world is facing a single urgent crisis with two dimensions: the degradation of the environment by global warming, pollution, depletion of resources, and the extinction of species; and the exploitation of human beings trapped in poverty and denied the secure setting needed for full personal development and a healthy communal life. While many commentators recognize these as separate problems, Francis insists that they are essentially united and organically connected so that they influence one another. The poor suffer most from environmental disasters. The hungry are hurt most by soil erosion. Marginalized people are most likely to become refugees due to climate change. By the same token, when people are lifted out of poverty, they can be more attentive to caring for their surroundings. When marginalized people are integrated into a healthy communal life, they can contribute to the crucial task of caring for our common home.

Recognizing that "all creatures are connected," an integral ecology is attuned to the mysterious "network of relations" between human beings and their environment. An integral approach promotes "human ecology," dedicated to creating a healthy communal life for all people, and an "environmental ecology," committed to caring for the earth and protecting it. Since the world is facing a single unified crisis with two interconnected aspects, we need to find comprehensive solutions that take both concerns into account.

In reading the signs of the times, Pope Francis detects a "decline in the quality of human life," the unruly growth of cities with "visual pollution and noise," and congested neighborhoods lacking in "green space." Technological innovations, which have accomplished much good, have also contributed to increased violence, social aggression, and drug trafficking. The omnipresent digital world can impede people from "learning how to live wisely, to think deeply and to love generously" (no. 47). The electronic world, which facilitates communication, can also "shield us from direct contact with the pain, the fears and the joys of others and the complexity of their personal experiences" (no. 47). The lack of physical encounters between the affluent powerful and the marginalized poor impoverishes both groups, leaving the poor invisible and the rich unmoved. In poor southern countries, "access to ownership of goods and resources for meeting vital needs is inhibited by a system of commercial relations and ownership which is structurally perverse" (no. 52). An integral ecology must be attentive to both the degradation of the earth and the cries of the poor.

Searching for the root causes of our united ecological problem, Francis assigns blame to what he calls "the technological paradigm," an undifferentiated one-dimensional way of viewing our relationship to the world which celebrates human control over material objects. This creates a confrontational relationship between the earth and human beings, who accept "the lie" that there is an infinite supply of the world's goods that can be "squeezed dry beyond every limit." In this outlook, the method and aims of science and technology become the only way of attaining truth and managing the world. Technology tends to absorb everything into its "ironclad logic," which seeks power and lordship over all. This paradigm celebrates the free market and economic growth without concern for its potentially negative impact on human beings and the natural world. Reliance on technology to solve our problems blinds us to the larger picture and more creative solutions. It creates a "consumerist mentality" that privileges having over being, placing greater value on accumulating possessions than on personal growth.

The pope insists that to "generate resistance to the assault of the technocratic paradigm" (no. 101), we need to think distinctively about public policies, educational programs, and various lifestyles. We might call this combination a "spiritual paradigm" that challenges the technocratic paradigm, or an ecological mindset that challenges the consumerist mindset.

A more spiritual approach to our ecological crisis can be grounded in a Christian anthropology. Francis teaches that humans are characterized by fundamental relationships to God, other persons, and nature. We are not God, and we did not create ourselves. We are totally dependent on the God who sustains us and is worthy of adoration. The Creator calls us to share in the ongoing task of creating our unfinished evolving world.

All human beings are made in the image and likeness of God, which means that we possess an inherent dignity, are worthy of respect, and have the right to be included in the community. As children of the Father, we are brothers and sisters to one another. All humans are always subjects and should never be reduced to objects. We must treat every other person as a *thou* and not as an *it*. As members of the human family, we are responsible for one another. Following the example and teachings of Jesus, we are to love our neighbor as ourselves, a command that extends to enemies as well as to those pushed to the margins and trapped in a circle of poverty. We are all members of a universal family—"a sublime communion" joined by "unseen hands"—that grounds our moral obligation to exclude no one from our compassion and care. This communion extends over time, creating an "intergenerational solidarity" that obliges us to care for the earth so that it is available in its beauty and richness for those who follow us.

Through our bodies we are organically related to the material world. We are members of the community of creatures. We come from the earth and return to it. The fate of the human family is essentially connected to the fate of the earth. The beauty of the natural world reveals to us something of the beauty of the Creator. As Francis puts it: "Rather than a problem to be solved, the world is a joyful mystery to be contemplated with gladness and praise" (no. 12). As Christians, our sense of being intimately connected to the earth is supported and focused by our belief in the Incarnation— that the Word became flesh in Jesus of Nazareth, who walked our earth and delighted in God's creation. Francis reinforces his major point: "There is no ecology without an adequate anthropology" (no. 118).

Some theologians argue that his position would be strengthened by including the common universe story shared by all humans. We are the product of a 13.7 billion–year history. We are stardust that has become conscious of itself. We are the leading edge of the evolutionary process, now responsible for its future progress. Even apart from this universe story, the relational anthropology espoused by Pope Francis provides a solid basis for an ecological spirituality that lives out the demands of loving our neighbor and protecting the earth.

In contrast to the technocratic paradigm, persons formed by Christian spirituality treat the earth not as material to be controlled and manipulated but as a gift from God worthy of respect and care. Realizing that material resources are finite, they try to limit their consumption and support sustainable development. Rejecting the common belief that accumulating possessions brings happiness, they try to simplify their lifestyle and make good with less. Persons with an ecological mindset are able to rise above the rugged individualism celebrated by our culture and make decisions based on concern for the common good, which Catholic Social Teaching describes as the sum total of conditions that allows humans to flourish. They reject unbridled forms of capitalism as well as dehumanizing forms of socialism in favor of economic systems and policies that serve the wellbeing of all the citizens, especially the most vulnerable and least fortunate. They are not content to remain in their own political and social enclaves but attempt to promote dialogue with those who are "other" and to make personal contact with them.

According to Francis, developing a spirituality that challenges the entrenched technocratic paradigm requires an "ecological conversion," a radical change of mind and heart, a new way of thinking and acting that combines care for the earth and love of the poor and powerless. To sustain this effort, we need "ecological virtues," habits formed by healthy family life, wise educational practices, socially responsible institutions, and, for Christians, a church attuned to the crisis of both the earth and the poor. Christians who have appropriated a spiritual paradigm can realistically face our urgent ecological crisis without losing "the joy of our hope" (no. 244). As Pope Francis reminds us at the end of his wide-ranging, beautifully written, faith-inspired encyclical: the Lord of life "does not abandon us, for his love constantly impels us to find new ways forward" (no. 245). In a final Christian prayer, the pope concludes, "The poor and the earth are crying out. O Lord, save us with your power and light, help us to protect all life, to prepare for a better future, for the coming of Your Kingdom of justice, peace, love and beauty. Praise be to You!"

Since the publication of *Laudato si'* in 2015, Pope Francis has made well-planned efforts to spread its urgent message. For example, in March 2020, he invited Catholic communities to participate in *"Laudato Si' Week"* from May 16 to 24 to celebrate its fifth anniversary and to encourage creative grassroots efforts to "take care of creation, a gift of our good Creator God."

A year later, Pope Francis launched a seven-year *"Laudato Si' Action Platform,"* which renewed his appeal to cultivate "respect for the gifts of the Earth and creation" and to "inaugurate a lifestyle and a society that is finally eco-sustainable."[13] Concerned about the next generation, the pope added: "From God's hands we have received a garden, we cannot leave a desert to our children." The pope's action platform has seven goals or areas of concern: "The response to the cry of the earth; the response to the cry of the poor; ecological economics; adoption of simple lifestyles; ecological education; ecological spirituality, and community engagement." Francis assigned this task to various institutions: families, parishes, schools, hospitals, businesses, organizations, and religious orders. In his announcement of the action platform, Pope Francis expressed hope that we can all collaborate, each in our own way, so that "our mother Earth may be restored to her original beauty and creation may once again shine according to God's plan."

Laudato si' provides one of our best examples of the preparation and background that goes into the CST documents. On October 4, 2023, the Feast of St. Francis of Assisi, Pope Francis published a relatively brief apostolic exhortation *Laudato deum* (*Praise God*) that was designed to encourage nations and individuals to do more to limit global warming. Eight years after publishing his lengthy encyclical *Laudato si'*, the pope issued this urgent warning that the response has not been adequate, and our planet is approaching a "point of no return" (no. 2). To the climate deniers, including those in the Catholic community, he repeats his claim that we can no longer doubt that global warming is caused by unchecked human intervention on nature in the past two centuries (no. 14). Once again, he blames the "technocratic paradigm" for propagating erroneous notions that human beings have no limits and can use the resources of the earth as they wish.

While recognizing that the most effective solutions must come from the developed nations of the world, Francis encourages all of us to do our part to reduce pollution and waste that will help create a new culture of care for creation that will eventually impact political decisions (nos. 70–91). The pope laments the lack of progress of the United Nations' climate conferences, but insists that losing hope would be "suicidal," exposing the human family, especially the poor and vulnerable, to the worst ravages of global warming.

I treat *Laudato deum* not as a separate document *but* as an important part of Pope Francis's ongoing effort to alert the Catholic community and the world to the environmental crisis and to prompt urgent action to save our common home.

Fratelli tutti (*On Fraternity and Social Friendship*)

Pope Francis published this encyclical in 2020 during the COVID-19 pandemic, which taught us that "no one can face life in isolation" and that we all need a community where we can support one another and dream together of a better future (no. 8). This encyclical is of special importance today because it not only names the dark forces that assail us, including armed conflicts that amount to a "third world war fought piecemeal," (no. 53) but also offers us "paths of hope" that fill our hearts and lift our spirits to the lofty realities of truth, goodness, beauty, justice, and love (no. 55).

In the second chapter, Pope Francis invites us to meditate on the parable of the Good Samaritan (Luke 10:25–37). He reminds us that those who failed to help the wounded man were religious persons who kept the first commandment by worshipping God but ignored the second commandment to love our neighbor. Throughout the chapter, Francis suggests various applications of the parable. It calls us to break barriers and build bridges. It invites us to create one great family where all can feel safe (cf. no. 62). It urges us to follow the example of the Good Samaritan and help form communities where members act as neighbors caring for vulnerable persons by lifting those who have fallen (cf. no. 63). It summons us to rediscover our vocation to form a society that serves the common good and respects every individual (cf. no. 66).

Fratelli tutti is also important because it calls us to follow Christ, the Prince of Peace, and do our part to spread his peace in our circle of influence. Francis reminds us that Christ never promoted violence and condemned the use of force to gain power over others. He admonished us to offer unlimited forgiveness to others (cf. Matt 18:22). The early Christian communities living in a corrupt pagan world sought to show respect to others with unfailing patience, to admonish opponents with gentleness, and to show every courtesy to everyone (cf. 2 Tim 2:25).

The pope offers us wise advice as we strive to be peacemakers: do not fuel anger or take revenge; cultivate virtues that promote reconciliation and solidarity (cf. no. 243); resolve conflicts through honest dialogue and patient negotiations (cf. no. 244); break the cycle of violence by forgiving perpetrators without denying the evil of the offense (cf. no. 251).

In a section on "The Injustice of War" (nos. 256–262), Pope Francis denounces war in stark terms: a "constant threat," an "assault on the environment," a "failure of politics and of humanity," a "shameful capitulation," a "stinging defeat before the forces of evil" (no. 261). Recognizing the immense power of weapons of mass destruction, the pope insists that we can no longer think of war as a solution. Furthermore, "it is very difficult nowadays to invoke the rational criteria elaborated in earlier centuries to speak of the possibility of a 'just war.'" For emphasis, the pope adds "never again war!" (no. 258).

As part of his dream for peace, Pope Francis calls the elimination of nuclear weapons a "moral and humanitarian imperative" (no. 262). He suggests that the money saved by defunding weapons be put in a "global fund" to eliminate hunger (no. 262). For Pope Francis, *Fratelli tutti* functions not as a definitive statement of doctrine but as a call to action and an invitation to dialogue.

2

THE SEVEN THEMES OF CATHOLIC SOCIAL TEACHING

In 1998, the United States Conference of Catholic Bishops (USCCB) published "Sharing Catholic Social Teaching: Challenges and Directions," which proposed seven themes found in the major CST documents. Since then, the U.S. bishops have added both brief and longer explanations. In the following commentaries, I have summarized the teaching of the bishops, added my own pastoral observations, and incorporated material from *Toward a Politics of Communion* by Anna Rowlands.[1]

Life and Dignity of the Human Person

The bishops state clearly that "the Catholic Church proclaims that human life is sacred and that the dignity of the human person is the foundation of a moral vision for society," a belief that grounds their social teaching. Among the attacks on human dignity, the bishops include abortion, euthanasia, the death penalty, arbitrary imprisonment, disgraceful working conditions, and war. They invite us to reflect on Jesus, who broke societal and religious customs by his respectful interaction with the Samaritan woman (John 4:1–42). Following Pope Francis, they call on us to recognize that our "throwaway culture" treats masses of people like things to be used and discarded, excluded, and easily forgotten. To invite personal reflection, the bishops pose the question: "Can we just stand by while people are starving?" We can also ask ourselves: In my daily interactions, who am I most likely to treat disrespectfully—a family member who disagrees with me on political issues, a friend who periodically disappoints me, a work colleague who does not do a good job, or a service worker who is socially challenged?

Professor Rowlands notes that the standard treatment of human dignity suffers from an overly individualistic account of human sin that concentrates on personal responsibility for evil actions while missing the powerful role of social sin and systemic evil. She applauds Gustavo Gutiérrez and other Latin American theologians for their groundbreaking analysis of social sin. Gutiérrez taught that personal sins get hardwired into cultural forms and embedded in social systems. This produces a "false consciousness," a distorted vision of the world that is blind to injustice and discrimination. The privileged do not recognize their advantages and expect the marginalized groups to accept their position in life. In this situation, it is the poor who recognize the dehumanizing effects of social sin they experience in their daily lives. As "experts by experience," they can lead the way in creating a more just and equitable world. Through a process of "raising consciousness," they can take charge of their own lives and become agents of change that humanize cultural traditions and societal practices.

The Conference of Latin American Bishops (CELAM) gave official recognition to this theology of social sin in their periodic meetings: Medellin in 1968; Puebla in 1969; and Aparecida in 2007. The bishops encouraged the formation of ecclesial base communities, small lay-led communities of prayer and reflection where marginalized persons can share their experiences of injustice and organize to improve their lot in life. Dr. Rowlands provides an analysis of human dignity that goes beyond fighting injustice and calls Christians to empower dispossessed persons to take hold of their own lives and contribute to the common good.[2]

Call to Family, Community, and Participation

The bishops begin with the statement, "Persons are not only sacred but also social"—a philosophical expression of a scriptural teaching. For example, the Apostle Paul writes: "We, who are many, are one body in

Christ, and individually we are members one of another" (Rom 12:5). The bishops call all of us to support the family, the "central social institution," the "most basic form of human community," the "small-scale church" where children can actualize their potential and develop Christian virtues. In this theme, the bishops propose the "principle of subsidiarity," the traditional norm for determining the scope and limits of governmental intervention. Government should not replace or destroy smaller communities and individual initiatives but should intervene only when it is necessary to help them flourish and contribute to the common good.

Dr. Rowlands offers an in-depth examination of "subsidiarity" briefly mentioned in the bishops' comments on this theme. In *Quadragesima anno*, his 1931 encyclical commemorating the fortieth anniversary of *Rerum novarum*, Pope Pius XI responded to significant world events: World War I, the rise of fascism in Italy and Germany, and economic depression affecting all countries. He was concerned that the modern state had become overburdened and increasingly ineffective, overwhelmed and submerged by endless efforts and responsibilities. At the same time, the growing evil of individualism had weakened associations and institutions that had historically enriched community life. Rowlands lists examples of such associations: trade unions, local governments, faith organizations, craft associations, football clubs, political parties, professional bodies, and charitable organizations.

In this situation, the principle of subsidiarity functions in two ways. First, it tries to limit the power of the state by insisting that it should intervene in local efforts only when necessary to promote the common good. While Pope Leo XIII had emphasized the proper role of the state in regulating economic affairs, Pius XI stressed the importance of curbing government interventions that were stifling the humanizing work of mediating institutions. For Pius XI, subsidiarity has a second function to revitalize associational life and empower smaller social groups. Rowlands envisions an ideal scenario in which the state is an "engaged player" enabling power to flow through various associations in a process that fosters social creativity and human dignity. In turn, fully functioning groups and associations contribute to the common good and take the pressure off the state to manage all societal problems.

Professor Rowlands summarizes how modern popes have applied the principle of subsidiarity. For example, John XXIII and Paul VI favored an expanded role of the state in providing welfare. John Paul II stressed the need to resist "bureaucratic and economic forms of tyranny." Benedict XVI saw subsidiarity as "the foremost way to foster freedom and responsibility." Pope Francis has spoken of subsidiarity as a "principle of hope" that maximizes participation and fosters responsibility.

Furthermore, Anna Rowlands points out that the sex abuse scandals in the Church demand further reflection on how small groups can be guilty of the abuse of power. As examples, she cites the L'Arche communities, Opus Dei, and the Legionnaires of Christ, where charismatic leaders offered bogus theological and spiritual justifications for abusive practices. Dr. Rowlands concludes that the principle of subsidiarity must include mechanisms for identifying, reporting, and resisting all authoritarian tendencies so that small communities can live their authentic charisms for the good of the Church and society.

Rights and Responsibilities

The bishops insist that protecting human rights and meeting responsibilities are essential to promoting human dignity and healthy communities. They invite us to reflect on the parable of the rich man who failed to see and meet the needs of the poor man, Lazarus (Luke 16:19–31). Human rights are under attack around the globe as one part of humanity lives in opulence and the other lives in poverty where their fundamental rights are ignored or violated, as Pope Francis observed in *Fratelli tutti*. The bishops also reference Pope Benedict XVI, who warned that individual rights detached from a "framework of duties" can "run wild," leading to an indiscriminate escalation of demands. In his 1963 encyclical, *Pacem in terris,* Pope John XXIII supported a series of human rights, including those necessary for a full human life: food, clothing, shelter, medical care, rest, and social services, adding that the state has the "duty to protect the rights of all its people," especially its weaker members. Today, it might be more accurate to say "society as a whole" has this duty, reminding all of us of our responsibility to protect human life and promote human flourishing.

In meeting their societal responsibilities, the large number of Catholic parishes, almost 1,800 dispersed around the country, make important contributions: providing quality education for inner-city students; collecting food and clothing for the needy; providing adult education on the moral perspectives of Catholic Social Teaching; joining with other groups to help neighborhoods provide a safe environment for young and old; promoting ecumenical efforts to limit gun violence; and providing hope for discouraged parishioners.

In her chapter on "the body politic," Professor Rowlands places the right to religious freedom in a social and political context.[3] She notes that it was Pope John XXIII, in *Pacem in terris*, who affirmed religious liberty as a fundamental human right for the first time. The pope paired this affirmation with an emphasis on corresponding society duties, which in tandem better serve the common good. For Rowlands, this means that religious liberty is best safeguarded in a "constitutional order of society" that promotes "communities of inquiry, teaching, formation, worship and charity."

In *Pacem in terris*, Pope John went beyond previous CST documents and spoke favorably of liberal democracy based on a written constitution and a separation of judicial, executive, and legislative powers. After *Pacem*, the choice for the Church was no longer between Christian monarchies and liberal democracy, but between totalitarianism and democracy.

Rowlands credits Vatican II with solidifying the right to religious liberty in its document *Dignitatis humanae*, which rooted this right in the dignity of the human person. Rowlands observes that the declaration "seeks to stress a narrative of continuity" that does not repudiate previous Catholic teaching but offers a "new articulation" of the way Catholics relate to political communities.

In this regard, it is helpful to recall the work of American theologian John Courtney Murray, SJ. Murray, who in the 1950s wrote scholarly articles arguing for religious liberty, was silenced by the Vatican in 1955 and forbidden from writing on that question. He complied, symbolically removing all his books on this topic from his room. After Pope John XXIII was elected, Murray was allowed to publish his book, *We Hold These Truths*, in 1960. When Vatican II commenced in 1962, Murray was not invited to attend as an expert, but in 1963, he was appointed an official expert at the urging of Cardinal Spellman. In that role Murray helped get religious liberty on the council agenda and became the primary writer of the third draft of *Dignitatis humanae*. After contentious debates the final draft with a few amendments was overwhelmingly adopted by the Council, officially accepting religious liberty as a human right based on the dignity of human beings.

Recalling Murray's long struggle to affirm religious liberty as a human right makes it difficult, if not impossible, to claim continuity in Church teaching. It seems obvious that the Church changed its position going from an explicit denial of religious liberty to an official conciliar affirmation of it as a human right. Over time, the Church came to a better understanding of the core message of Christ and its implications for a changing world. This is the same process that resulted in other changes in Church teaching on usury, slavery, and most recently capital punishment. With its late but important affirmation of religious liberty, the Church is in a better position to proclaim and defend other important human rights under attack around the world.

Option for the Poor and Vulnerable

The U.S. bishops embraced the theme developed by Latin American theologians known as the "preferential option for the poor." In our society threatened by deepening divisions between rich and poor, the bishops invite us to reflect on the story of the Last Judgment where Jesus identifies himself with the hungry, the thirsty, and the imprisoned (Matt 25:31–46). They cite Pope Francis, who insists the poor have a "leading role" to play in their own liberation by expressing their own "feelings, choices and ways of living and working." Referencing Pope John Paul II, the bishops point out that the Church's love for the poor is a "constant tradition based on the lived poverty of Jesus, his Sermon on the Mount and his personal love for marginalized persons in his society." The "option for the poor" is not an "adversarial slogan" that pits the poor against the rich. It is a call to empower the poor so that they can become "active participants in the life of society," joining with others in contributing to the common good. Today, Catholics have an effective way of assisting the poor by contributing to the Catholic Campaign for Human Development, which funds self-help programs that provide jobs for people looking not for a handout but a way out of the hellish circle of poverty.

In his seminal work, *A Theology of Liberation*, Peruvian theologian Gustavo Gutiérrez argues that the preferential option for the poor is not Marxist ideology but rather a "Christian practice" based on Scripture read from the perspective of marginalized people. In the Exodus, God freed the Israelites from the cruel fate of slaves and blessed them with personal and social freedom. Jesus Christ, who lived under Roman oppression, presented himself as sent by God to liberate captives and preach the good news to the poor (Luke 4:18–19). He identified himself with the needy and taught us to love our neighbor by concrete acts of charity. Gutiérrez described theology as a critical reflection on *praxis*, that is, purposeful activities designed to overcome injustice. This shifts the emphasis from traditional orthodoxy (correct doctrine) to "orthopraxis" (correct practices). For Gutiérrez, living the gospel faithfully is even more important than defining doctrines accurately.

Commenting on the preferential option for the poor, Dr. Rowlands affirms the groundbreaking work of Latin American liberation theologians on social sin and analyzes the reluctance of the Vatican to accept this notion. Pope John Paul II argued that only individual persons can sin and no institution can be a moral agent. Faced with unjust situations, human beings remain free to resist evil and do good in cooperation with God's grace. Rowlands notes that John Paul acknowledged that unjust structures can create incentives to personal sin, but he never recognized the preferential role that marginalized people play in identifying and resisting the evil consequences of social sin. In this regard, we should add that Cardinal Ratzinger, as head of the Congregation for the Doctrine of the Faith, warned against an uncritical use of the phrase "preferential option for the poor" because of its connections with various currents of Marxist thought. Dr. Rowlands concludes her analysis of social sin by observing that the Vatican and liberation theologians have proceeded along different paths without ever completing the task of producing a comprehensive, compelling Catholic narrative of the social and structural dimensions of sin—which, I might add, makes it more difficult for pastors to convince the faithful to accept the preferential option for the poor.

The Dignity of Work and the Rights of Workers

Drawing from Scripture, this theme presents work as our way of participating in God's ongoing creation. To protect the dignity of workers, society must recognize the rights of workers to productive work, to fair wages, to join unions, to private property, and to economic initiative. Through work, human beings cultivate their gifts and talents, contribute to the development of society, and provide sustenance for their families. Therefore, it is essential to "prioritize the goal of access to steady employment for everyone." Providing the poor with financial assistance must always be a "provisional solution" while pursuing the broader objective of providing them with a job leading to a "dignified life."

Referencing Pope Benedict, the bishops reminded governments that their citizens are the "primary capital to be self-guided and valued." Economic systems must be "structured and governed" so they promote the dignity of workers and their labors. Reflecting on this theme can generate various responses: expressions of gratitude for having meaningful work; returning to school to prepare for better employment; deciding to retire to enjoy more leisure time; locating financial assistance for an unemployed relative; devising creative ways of finding meaning in toilsome jobs; and expressing personal views on minimum wage issues to a congressional representative.

In a section on "an integral ecology" of work,[4] Rowlands expands the bishops' teachings by highlighting work as a "vocation" that is never a mere "transactional arrangement" but a "reciprocal exchange," through which we became our moral selves. She points out that the monastic tradition insists that physical labor is important to the contemplative life and that personal growth comes from a fruitful interplay between recollection and work. To avoid making an idol out of work, a balanced life must include time for leisure. She goes on to recognize that CST has the difficult task of upholding the high value of work without sanctioning or promoting what we might call "workaholism."

Rowlands warns against an excessively "rosy" understanding of human work that neglects the biblical account of the fall that turned the blessings of pleasurable work into the curse of arduous toil. She argues that this aspect of work highlights the need for good labor unions to support workers burdened with toilsome tasks. To be pastorally effective, CST must view work as both blessing and curse in an effort to make human labor more productive and less burdensome.

Solidarity

The bishops present solidarity as a virtue that strengthens us as "one human family" and as the keepers of our brothers and sisters in the pursuit of justice and peace in our shrinking world. They invite us to reflect on relevant scriptural passages: for example, in a section on the Body of Christ, the Apostle Paul writes: "If one member suffers, all suffer together with it; if one member is honored, all rejoice together with it" (1 Cor 12:26). The bishops recognize that, in today's world, the sense of solidarity is being replaced by a "deceptive illusion" that we are "all-powerful individuals" on a solitary journey, propelled by the "empire of money," as Pope Francis expressed it in *Fratelli tutti* (no. 30). The virtue of solidarity can be practiced by consumers who realize that purchasing is not only an economic act but also a "moral act." We can imagine various ways of practicing the moral virtue of solidarity in our purchasing habits: buying produce from local farmers; limiting the purchase of luxury items and donating the money to charity; buying only what is needed so goods do not go to waste; and budgeting money for Church and charities before other expenses.

In a dense informative chapter on solidarity, Rowlands places CST on solidarity in the context of secular solidarity movements for civil, racial, and gender rights.[5] In this regard, she highlights the role of Pope John Paul, who not only described solidarity as a Christian virtue but also supported Poland's Solidarity Labor movement and its role in overthrowing the communist regime. In the Christian tradition, solidarity is rooted in our vertical relationship with Christ who calls us to a close horizontal relationship with our neighbors and the whole of creation. Modern socialist movements, however, have promoted solidarity as a totally secular project to replace the ineffective Christian approach based on love. Nevertheless, Rowlands claims that the secular and Christian approaches to solidarity engaged in an informal mutually critical dialogue in the 1930s that enriched the development of CST for the rest of the century and beyond.

Rowlands traces this development through the teachings of the popes. For example, Pope John employed solidarity as an "engine" to promote the common good and world peace. In its main social document, *Gaudium et spes*, Vatican II taught that we are saved as members of the people of God and that the Church is a "community of solidarity" called to be a sign and instrument of God's saving work in the world. Pope John Paul established solidarity as a permanent principle of CST that produces justice and peace as its fruit. Pope Benedict insisted that solidarity builds trust necessary for the effective functioning of economic markets. Finally, Rowlands notes various contributions of Pope Francis: expanding the notion of solidarity to include care for creation and a commitment to sustainable development; using solidarity as the framework for his entire encyclical *Fratelli tutti*; and inviting us to a "mystical contemplation" of our intimate communion with God our Father and Christ our brother leading to a genuine sense of solidarity with all God's creatures.

Care for God's Creation

The bishops provide a brief exposition of this seventh and last theme, stressing that our faith reminds us to be good "stewards" of creation, protecting our planet and its inhabitants. For further guidance, we can recall the teaching of *Laudato si'*, published by Pope Francis in 2015 with the subtitle, *Care for Our Common Home*. As we saw in the first chapter, Francis accepted the scientific consensus that global warming is an imminent threat to the earth and wrote his encyclical to convince countries to support the Paris Agreement to limit the emission of greenhouses gases. Since then, the pope has continued to urge everyone to limit their carbon output. We can do our part in various ways: limit driving by walking more and using public transportation; eat more fruits and vegetables and less red meat; compost food waste; bring reusable bags when shopping; use less water bathing and showering; and in many other ways suggested by U.S. environmental groups.

This theme has special relevance and urgency today, since God's creation is facing such grave threats from floods, wildfires, hurricanes, and other natural disasters. As the threat of global warming becomes more evident, let us join Pope Francis in the prayer he offers to conclude *Laudato si'*: "All-powerful God, you are present in the whole universe and the smallest of your creatures…press upon us the power of your love, that we may protect life and beauty. Amen."

In a chapter dealing with environmental problems, Rowlands once again turns to Pope Francis, who challenges our "practices of high consumption" and "rapid growth" that lead to economic inequalities and indifference to the environment.[6] In *Laudato si'*, the pope invites us to see creation in all its beauty and diversity as a "sign of the goodness of the Creator" and as a "gift from the outstretched hand of the Father of all." To highlight the moral significance of this faith conviction, Rowlands draws on the CST principle "the universal destination of goods." The earth is a "shared inheritance," and its fruits are meant to benefit all, which in our world of increasing inequalities demands the preferential option for the poor. Pope Francis, who often asserts that "all things are connected," insists that we are facing a single urgent crisis with two dimensions: degradation of the environment and the exploitation of human beings trapped in poverty, both of which require a unified theological, moral, and spiritual response. Concretely, Francis encourages us to discover God in all things—"in a leaf, a mountain trail, a dew drop, and a poor person's face." Summing up the message of Pope Francis, Rowlands insists that an effective response to our ecological crisis requires an "integral ecology" that includes a "mystical vison" of creation as a gift from God and an "ethical obligation" to create a just world where no one is excluded from its abundance.[7]

3

PASTORAL LETTERS AND STATEMENTS OF THE U.S. CATHOLIC BISHOPS

Pope Francis has reminded us of the importance of pastoral letters issued by national conferences of bishops by frequently referencing them. Since 1917, the U.S. bishops have organized themselves under various names, eventually settling in 2001 on the United States Conference of Catholic Bishops (USCCB). During the early years of our republic, the bishops were generally silent on public issues, even the great moral issue of slavery. During the twentieth century, the bishops became much more vocal, writing well-publicized pastorals in the 1980s on peace and the economy. Later that decade, the USCCB also attempted to write a pastoral letter on women that proved to be extremely contentious. After consultations initiated by the Vatican and several rewrites, a fourth draft failed to gain the needed two-thirds vote to pass at the USCCB meeting in 1992, and the project was abandoned. In 1998, Pope John Paul issued a document declaring that bishops conferences must have unanimous consent of their members to teach in the name of the Church, a ruling that has made it virtually impossible for the USCCB to publish any more pastoral letters on controversial public issues.

Bishops' Program of Social Reconstruction (1919)

At the close of World War I on February 12, 1919 (Abraham Lincoln's birthday), the American bishops published this groundbreaking document that included concrete proposals for creating a more just and humane society. In his singularly informative book, *Catholic Social Teaching and Movements*, activist and scholar Marvin Mich examined the genesis of this important document, highlighting the indispensable role of Msgr. John Ryan (1869–1945). Ryan, a son of Irish immigrants, was ordained as a priest of the Diocese of St. Paul in 1898 and earned a doctorate in theology from the Catholic University of America in 1906, where he later taught from 1915 until 1939. He published his revised dissertation, which argued for a federal minimum wage, under the title "A Living Wage." During his studies, Ryan became very familiar with Pope Leo XIII's encyclical *Rerum novarum* and made it his life's work explaining and adapting it to the American situation.

Without extensive consultation, Ryan wrote the "Bishops' Program of Social Reconstruction," which the bishops accepted without any changes and published as their own. It begins by putting its teaching in historical context: "The ending of the Great War has brought peace. But the only safeguard of peace is social justice and a contented people." In part three of the document, Ryan listed a series of "desirable and attainable" concrete proposals as a way of "translating our faith into works." For example, he proposed minimum wage legislation, social insurance to protect injured and unemployed workers, child labor laws, labor's right to organize and bargain collectively, public housing for the urban poor, progressive taxation, regulation of monopolies, and government control of utilities.

Professor Mich also provides helpful commentary on the reception of the reconstruction program, noting that while Ryan maintained his proposals were both "traditional and conservative" and a reasonable, creative adaptation of *Rerum novarum* to the American scene, readers tended to see them as "innovative and radical," probably because Leo XIII's encyclical was still not known nor understood in the United States nearly thirty years after its publication. Part of the novelty was that the American bishops, who were generally regarded as caught up in internal church affairs, had now for the first time inserted themselves into the public life of the nation. According to Mich, the failure of American Catholics to understand Ryan's work was "fortuitous" because it prompted the bishops to initiate a series of programs to educate the faithful in the social thought of the Church and to establish a Social Action Department to organize an effort to bring Catholic Social Teaching to bear upon social legislation before Congress. This lobbying function has become a regular part of the public ministry of the USCCB—a fitting legacy of Msgr. John Ryan, who dreamed of a constructive dialogue between Catholic moral teaching and the American ideal of forming a more perfect union.

The Challenge of Peace (1983)

The American bishops published this pastoral letter in 1983 as a response to the crisis created by the development of nuclear weapons that, as they noted in the opening paragraph, "drastically changed the nature of warfare" and led to an unprecedented arms race that posed a threat to human life and all that we hold dear.

When Ronald Reagan was elected president in 1980, he advocated a massive arms buildup, including nuclear weapons, and a more militant stand against the Soviet Union that had invaded Afghanistan in 1979. At the November 1980 meeting of the American bishops, Bishop Francis Murphy, auxiliary bishop of Baltimore and a member of Pax Christi, suggested that the conference should address the morality of nuclear weapons. This intervention led to the establishment of a committee of bishops—Tom Gumbleton, John O'Connor, David Reilly, and George Fulcher—chaired by Joseph Bernardin, Archbishop of Cincinnati.

Initiating a new methodology, the committee began by holding fourteen public hearings, gathering information from seventy-six witnesses, including a cabinet secretary, scripture scholars, and peace activists. This led to the publication of a first draft in June 1982 that drew strong criticisms from Archbishop Phillip Hannan, who wanted to scrap the whole project because it would harm U.S. negotiations with the Soviets. Nevertheless, the committee went ahead and published a second draft in October 1983 that gained more secular attention and landed Archbishop Bernardin on the cover of *Time* magazine.

A third draft was proposed for the May 1983 meeting of the bishops' conference which called for a "halt" to testing, production, and employment of nuclear weapons. Bishop O'Connor introduced an amendment to change the word "halt" to "curb," a position influenced by the Vatican and supported by the Reagan Administration. Archbishop John Quinn of San Francisco and a Pax Christi bishop argued that "curb" would not stop the dangerous arms race and would allow the development of new nuclear weapons systems. The final version, which returned to the word "halt," was approved by a vote of 238 to 9 and was promulgated on May 3, 1983.

In their opening summary of *The Challenge of Peace*, the bishops in their teaching distinguished between universally binding moral principles and specific applications that allowed for "diversity of opinion." In a section on peace in the Scriptures, they pointed out that because we have been gifted with God's peace in the risen Christ, we are called to making peace in our world (no. 55).

In discussing the morality of war, the bishops drew on their interpretation of the traditional just war criteria for deciding when the strong presumption against war can be overridden (cf. nos. 85–110): *Just Cause*—to protect innocent life and secure basic human rights; not as retribution; *Competent Authority*—war must be declared by legitimate authority, those responsible for public order; *Comparative Justice*— challenges both sides to recognize the limits of their "just cause" and to ask if the rights and values that are in conflict justify the taking of human life; *Right Intention*—related to just cause and the pursuit of moral order as the basis of peace, it challenges unnecessarily destructive acts or imposing unreasonable conditions, such as unconditional surrender; *Last Resort*—all peaceful alternatives must have been exhausted; *Probability of Success*—questions the irrational resort of force or hopeless resistance, yet it also leaves room for "proportionate" witness to key values; *Proportionality*—the damage to be inflicted and the costs incurred by war must be proportionate to the good expected by taking up arms.

While employing the just war criteria in their moral judgments, the bishops endorsed pacifism, the Christian tradition of nonviolence, as an option for individuals but not as a duty or obligation for countries or individuals.

On the morality of the U.S. policy of Mutual Assured Destruction (MAD), the bishops took a position of "conditional acceptance," judging the policy "morally acceptable" as a step on the way toward progressive disarmament. It cannot be a long-term basis for peace, which must not be based on "equality of arms" but on "mutual trust." The bishops concluded their peace pastoral with a confession that it is our belief in the

41

risen Christ, who will never fail us, that sustains us in confronting the awesome challenge of the nuclear arms race (cf. no. 339).

Empowered by the Spirit: Campus Ministry Faces the Future (1985)

While spending three years as the writer for the editorial committee that drafted this pastoral letter, I learned a good deal about the dynamics of producing such a document as well as the language and content needed to win approval of the bishops' conference. After *Empowered by the Spirit* was published, I spent a good deal of time and energy spreading its message and suggestions, especially the proposal to establish "Chairs of Catholic Thought" at universities including Kentucky, Cincinnati, and New Mexico. This experience reinforced my conviction to include *Empowered by the Spirit* in a list of CST documents, especially the section on "Educating for Justice" that has made such an impact on many U.S. collegians (cf. nos. 70–82).

In that section, the bishops insist that the Church on campus be a "consistent and vigorous advocate for justice, peace and reverence for all life" (no. 73) based on the transcendence of God and the dignity of the human person (no. 74). They call special attention to the "coherent body of Catholic Social Thought" that should inform the work for justice. Recognizing the power of social sin, the bishops call the Church on campus to "empower individuals and groups to take charge of their own lives and to shape their own destinies" (no. 76). In an especially consequential paragraph, the pastoral urges campus ministers to get students involved in various Christian service projects that involve theological reflection on their service experience "designed to encourage them to be life-long seekers after justice" (no. 79).

For over thirty years, *Empowered by the Spirit* informed and guided the training and programing of Catholic campus ministry touching millions of future leaders of society and church. Still today, Christian service projects that involve encounters with poor persons close to home and abroad are extremely popular on Catholic colleges and universities, providing direct experience of social sin and the opportunity to learn from marginalized persons. For example, Fordham University in New

York reports that in a recent year their students contributed well over a million hours of volunteer service. At the University of Dayton, a Marianist institution in Ohio, campus ministry sponsors a vibrant Center for Social Concerns that provides students with multiple opportunities for participating in Christian service projects, including day-long immersion experiences in local poverty areas and longer encounters with marginal groups in Latin America. Of course, not every student volunteer takes advantage of the learning opportunity, not every Christian service project includes theological reflection that applies CST principles, and not every service program is initiated by campus ministry. Nevertheless, a good case can be made that *Empowered by the Spirit* has done more to spread the understanding and practice of CST than any other USCCB pastoral letter.

Furthermore, the success of *Empowered by the Spirit* suggests that CST can increase its impact by informing the practice of established institutions—for example, seminary formation, continuing education for priests and deacons, curricula of collegiate theology departments, diocesan continuing education programs, and especially preaching and programming in the vast network of parishes where Catholics learn and practice their faith.

Economic Justice for All (1986)

This pastoral letter is of special interest for the process that produced it and the reception it received. In the resource book *Modern Catholic Social Teaching*, moral theologian Charles Curran summarized the development of the document. A committee of five bishops headed by Rembert Weakland of Milwaukee was charged with writing a draft examining the U.S. economy from a moral perspective. They began by holding a series of meetings to hear the views of economists, sociologists, business and labor leaders, theologians, and social justice activists. At the same time, they welcomed correspondence from the public.

In 1984 and again in 1985 they made public preliminary drafts of the proposed document, which generated a good deal of attention from secular media as well as religious outlets. The final document did not endorse any specific economic system but proposed moral principles to reform the U.S. economy, primarily the fundamental moral criterion that economic decisions must serve all people, especially the poor. Drawing on Scripture and traditional Catholic Social Teaching, the pastoral stressed the dignity and rights of persons, the social nature of human existence, the quest for economic justice, and the importance of special care for the least fortunate in society. The letter pointed out the great social dangers posed by unbridled individualism and called for cooperative efforts to improve the economy. The bishops argued that society as a whole will benefit if we remember that our economic system should be judged by what it does to and for people.

Despite the initial publicity given the drafts of EJA, the final version had a limited impact. For example, leading economic journals virtually ignored it. Economists who espouse value-free approaches simply dismissed it as irrelevant. Some conservative business leaders judged it impractical. Many priests did not even mention it in the pulpit. Although the bishops budgeted over $500,000 for a well-designed implementation plan, the pastoral never exercised the kind of influence envisioned by its supporters. One survey taken a year after its publication found that only about 30 percent of adult Catholics had even heard about it, let alone read it.

Nevertheless, the pastoral did make some limited impact. Milton Friedman said it moved him to clarify his own moral assumptions. The University of Notre Dame, among others, introduced courses dealing directly with the pastoral. James O'Leary, a former vice-chairman of the board of United Trust Company, stated publicly that the document brought about a conversion in his life and could do the same for others.

The pastoral was attacked from both the left and the right. Democratic socialists like Michael Harrington argued that the letter failed to propose the kind of radical solutions needed to revive our ailing economy. Neoconservatives led by Michael Novak demonstrated their displeasure by issuing their own statement, "Liberty and Justice for All," which offers a much more positive view of the U.S. economy and puts greater emphasis on productivity than on redistribution of wealth. Conservative commentators charged that the pastoral called for governmental solutions to all our problems. Supporters countered by pointing out the crucial distinction made by the pastoral between state and society, meaning that all segments of society are responsible for improving the economy and not just the state or government. Some commentators noted that the criticisms from both sides indicated that the letter was a reformist document that accepted the general mix of free market and state control currently existing in the United States, while calling for vigorous efforts to overcome existing injustices and inequities.

The bishops' pastoral also sparked a discussion of whether human beings possess economic rights in addition to the traditional political and social rights guaranteed by the Constitution. The pastoral, for instance, spoke of the right to a job with adequate pay and called for a new national commitment for securing such rights for everyone. Critics denied that human beings possess such positive economic rights, arguing that this would mean that some entity has the corresponding obligation to provide for these rights. They feared that talk of economic rights would move people to expect the government to take care of all their material needs and diminish their sense of self-reliance. Proponents countered that most people want to work rather than rely on state welfare. Securing jobs for workers is not an act of charity but of justice that enables them to actualize themselves and contribute to society. It is the responsibility not of the government alone, but of the whole society to secure economic rights for all.

The religious vision presented in the pastoral letter sharpened the debate between economists like Milton Friedman, who espouse economic individualism, and sociologists like Robert Bellah, who emphasize the revival of public virtues and concern for the common good. Strenuously objecting to the bishops' moral stance, Friedman, on the one hand, insisted that only individuals possess moral obligations and duties not societies or governments. He argued that the freedom of individuals to pursue their own economic interests is the best way to produce a healthy economy benefiting all.

On the other hand, Bellah argued against the common American assumption that the economy is an autonomous realm that should be allowed to run on its own without any external interference. He called this is a "dangerous myth" and a clear example of false consciousness. For him, the free market fueled by competition and an acquisitive spirit enables corporations to engage in questionable practices, such as closing factories without notice and putting undue pressure on employees. Bellah insisted that we can overcome such limitations in our economy only by recovering a concern for the common good and by inculcating the public virtues associated with good citizenship. The bishops made an important contribution, according to Bellah, by insisting that participation and solidarity are more important than competition and survival in creating a more humane economy.

Today, *Economic Justice for All* is seldom explicitly referenced even by Catholic theologians. However, recalling its extensive preparation as well as its mixed reception reminds us that we are all responsible in our own limited way for creating a more just and equitable world.

Renewing the Earth (1991)

In this pastoral letter on the environment, the Catholic bishops of the United States emphasized an approach that we can call "prophetic." They insisted on a consistent respect for human life that includes care for the created world. The whole human family is interdependent, and all of us must work for the common good. A contemporary "ethics of solidarity" requires an equitable use of resources and a special care for the poor and the outcasts. An authentic ecological spirituality must recognize the limits of material growth and the need for people in the industrialized countries to curb consumption. For the bishops, it is fundamentally unjust for the industrialized North, which constitutes less than 20 percent of the world's population, to consume 75 percent of the earth's natural resources.

The prophetic approach of the U.S. bishops highlights the notion of stewardship. Human beings are called not to dominate the earth but to tend the global garden as good stewards. According to the book of Genesis, God settled Adam in the garden of Eden to cultivate and care for it (Gen 2:15). This remains the ongoing task of the human family. Prophetic ecology rejects environmental exploitation based on Genesis 1, which speaks of human mastery of the animal world and the divine command to fill the earth and conquer it. It makes stewardship, rather than domination, the central category. As human beings we are in charge of the material world, but we must carry out this responsibility with care and respect. The prophetic approach embraces an enlightened anthropocentrism that places human beings in the center of creation while insisting that we take responsibility for its well-being. We are not merely one of many species inhabiting the earth. We are the leading edge of the evolutionary process and have the privileged task of guiding it to its ultimate fulfillment.

Prophetic ecology supports an environmental ethic with pragmatic arguments that appeal to sober realists. We must be reasonable stewards in order to maintain the earth as a habitable place for the human family. We must reject consumerism, waste, and exploitation so that the earth can continue to sustain coming generations. The good of all demands that the industrialized countries help the developing nations gain access to their fair share of the world's goods.

Benedict of Nursia, who founded the first Benedictine monastery at Monte Cassino, Italy, in 529, serves as a fitting patron saint of prophetic ecology. During the Middle Ages, the Benedictine monks cleared the land, developed sanitation systems, and refined agricultural methods. They lived a simple lifestyle, and their communities were economically self-sustaining. Although our postmodern world is very different from theirs, the Benedictine emphasis on simplicity, practical care of the earth, and sustainable economic systems can certainly help us respond to the current environmental crisis.

The Harvest of Justice Is Sown in Peace (1993)

Following the end of the Cold War in 1991, violent conflicts based on ethnic, racial, and religious differences multiplied around the world, including the well-publicized war in Bosnia and the barely noticed tribal warfare in Burundi. These local conflicts raised a new set of complex moral questions. For example, what can the United States do to help prevent more of these conflicts from arising in the future? When is it fitting for us to intervene for humanitarian purposes? What means should be used to control the violence?

In November 1993, on the tenth anniversary of the publication of the pastoral letter, *The Challenge of Peace*, the Catholic bishops of the United States issued this public statement that offered useful guidance on these questions. Inspired by traditional Catholic Social Teaching, the statement urged our government to increase its support for the United Nations so that it can play its proper role of reducing conflict in the world. An effective multilateral United Nations "can relieve the United

States of the burden, or the temptation, of becoming by itself the world's police force." While recognizing that the UN system will have to become stronger and more efficient to play its proper peacekeeping role, the bishops argued that, in the long run, the United States can best respond to regional conflicts within a multinational framework.

The bishops insisted that U.S. foreign policy can help prevent regional conflicts by working to secure human rights for all. Emerging democracies flourish best on the solid base of civil, political, social, cultural, and economic rights for every individual and all groups. Our country should help to establish international arrangements that protect the poor and vulnerable. According to the bishops, guaranteeing human rights is "an indispensable condition for a just and peaceful world order."

The Harvest of Justice maintained a balanced perspective on the religious dimension of local conflicts. On the one hand, the bishops asserted that every violent act in the name of religion is a "crime against God and a scandal for religious believers." On the other hand, they claimed that the "instances of religion being the principal cause of conflict are extremely rare." Quite the contrary, authentic religious belief has been a powerful moral force for achieving human liberation in many places, including Central America, Eastern Europe, South Africa, and the Philippines. Reflecting the traditional Christian ideal of unity-in-diversity, the bishops insisted that commitment to a particular religious tradition should include a concern for the universal common good.

The bishops proposed economic sanctions as a way of combating aggression of injustice without resorting to military intervention or falling into passivity. Recognizing that sanctions often hurt innocent persons and can be counterproductive, they offer some tentative criteria for deciding when to impose them. First, comprehensive economic sanctions should be considered only in response to "grave and ongoing injustices" and after less serious measures have failed. Second, the good achieved by the sanctions should outweigh the harm caused—a principle that rules out denying the fundamental necessities of life to the civilian population. Third, substantial portions of the affected population should consent to the sanctions. Finally, sanctions should always be part of a broader diplomatic effort to find political solutions. Economic sanctions that adhere to these norms can be effective. For example, they helped overturn the apartheid policy in South Africa.

The Harvest of Justice also took up the immensely complex issue of military intervention in the internal affairs of other countries for humanitarian purposes. The extreme violence, injustice, and chaos in countries such as Haiti, Bosnia, Liberia, Iraq, Somalia, Sudan, and Burundi raised difficult moral questions about humanitarian intervention. In response, the bishops aligned themselves with Pope John Paul II, who urged that "humanitarian intervention be obligatory where the survival of populations and entire ethnic groups is seriously compromised."[1] According to the pope, when "populations are succumbing to the attacks of an unjust aggressor," nations no longer have a "right to indifference." But in order to avoid "new forms of imperialism or endless wars of altruism,"[2] the American bishops placed this call for humanitarian intervention in a larger moral context. We are members of one human family and cannot be indifferent to any suffering within the family. National sovereignty is an important, but not absolute, good. The principle of nonintervention can be overridden in cases of genocide or when whole populations are threatened by aggression or anarchy.

Nonmilitary intervention such as humanitarian aid and economic sanctions should take priority over the use of force. Decisions about military interventions should be based on just war norms, especially on whether there is a good possibility of achieving a just and stable peace, and whether the good intended outweighs the suffering caused by the use of force. The right of a powerful country like the United States to intervene in other nations must be carefully circumscribed by international law and global ethics. Multilateral interventions authorized by the United Nations are preferable to unilateral approaches that can lead to imperialistic abuses. At the same time, the bishops recognized that the United States, as the only remaining superpower, bore a special responsibility to overcome injustice and to assist oppressed people. *The Harvest of Justice* closed with a reminder that "our peacemaking vocation is not a passing priority, a cause for a decade, but an essential part of our mission to proclaim the Gospel and renew the earth."

Open Wide Our Hearts (2018)

To combat the rise of racist incidents in our country, the USCCB published this pastoral letter in 2018, building on their previous 1979 pastoral, *Brothers and Sisters to Us*. In a section called "What Is Racism?," the bishops define racism as thinking one's own race is superior and others are inferior. Racist acts are sinful because they violate justice and charity, failing to acknowledge the dignity of others as brothers and sisters made in God's image. Racism is manifested in various ways: public displays of symbols of hatred like nooses; discrimination in housing, education, and incarceration; allocation of resources (for example, the Flint water crisis); police practices (for example, driving while Black); and sins of omission (for example, failure to speak out against racial injustice). The bishops recognize progress made in civil rights but note that "racism still profoundly affects our culture," causing "great harm to its victims and corrupting the souls of those who harbor racist or prejudicial thoughts." In this situation, we need a "conversion of heart" leading to institutional and societal reforms.

Open Wide Our Hearts formats its responses based on Micah 6:8 which says the Lord requires us to do justice, to love kindness, and to walk humbly with our God. Under "Doing Justice," the bishops admit that our nation has done little to acknowledge the harm done by racism to so many: "No means of atonement, no natural process of reconciliation, and all too often a neglect of our history." They recount the experiences of various groups: Native Americans, who were killed, enslaved, and relocated by European explorers; African Americans, who were subjected to chattel slavery, denied their constitutional rights as citizens, and subjected to ongoing violence (more than 400 were lynched between 1877 and 1950); and Hispanics, who have known discrimination in housing, employment, healthcare, and education. At the end of this section, the bishops admit that we have not sufficiently examined how racist attitudes of yesterday have become a permanent part of our perceptions, practices, and policies today, "enshrined in our social, political, and economic structures."

In a section called "Loving Goodness," the pastoral letter encourages us to follow Christ's command to love our neighbor, which requires us to "make room for others in our hearts" and to see others as our brothers and sisters. Christian love compels us to "resist racism courageously," to reach out generously to the victims of this evil, to assist the conversion of those who harbor racist attitudes, and to begin to change policies and structures that allow racism to persist.

As an example of "loving goodness," the bishops raise Augustus Tolton (d. 1897), a former slave who overcame harsh discrimination to become the first Black priest born in the United States. They also cite St. Katharine Drexel (d. 1955), who founded many schools for Native and Black Americans. In urging Christians to manifest joy in serving God and neighbor, she used the phrase "let us open wide our hearts," providing the title of this pastoral letter.

In the final section, "Walk Humbly with God," the bishops urge us to acknowledge that the Church has been complicit in racism in various ways. For example, in 1452, Pope Nicolas V granted permission to the kings of Spain and Portugal to buy and sell Africans into slavery. During the Civil War, many bishops refused to condemn slavery and some even owned slaves. Catholic parishes in Washington, DC were still segregated in the 1940s, with Black parishioners relegated to the back pews and directed to approach the communion rail only after all the white parishioners had received communion.

In an extremely consequential move, the bishops who have consistently condemned abortion, euthanasia, and assisted suicide as forms of violence that threaten human life, purposely added to this list, "We unequivocally state that racism is a life issue," adding that we pledge to work toward ending racism that violates the dignity inherent in each person.

Open Wide Our Hearts found a mixed reception. Commentators have suggested that it was a step in the right direction and a needed reminder of our duty to combat racism. The *National Catholic Reporter* praised it as a worthy addition to previous statements and "a solid introductory teaching document," especially on the history of racism.[3] Franciscan theologian Daniel Horan noted that "much of what was said is good," but criticized it for failing to identify the perpetrators of racism, including those who enjoy white privilege "blissfully unaware" of their complicity in "structures of oppression."[4] Some commentators have joined Horan in this criticism, while others think the bishops were wise to bypass this very controversial issue of white privilege.

Open Wide Our Hearts deserves attention today as U.S. educators debate how to teach the history of racism in our country. By combining confession of racial sins with a pledge to overcome racism, the U.S. bishops suggest an approach to dealing with our national history of racial prejudice and practice. As a nation, we must face the harsh reality of our long history of racism, not as a misguided exercise leading to a false sense of personal and collective guilt, but as a necessary first step paving the way for constructive efforts to create a more just society.

We teach students that slavery dehumanized both masters and slaves so that they might be more attentive to the dangers posed today by racial inequality in our society. We tell the story of our "original sin" as a prelude to celebrating God's more powerful healing grace. We recount the horrors of slavery and the criminal failures of reconstruction to strengthen our commitment to work for racial justice that celebrates the victories of the civil rights movement as signs of hope that further progress can be made. An honest portrayal of our racial history is necessary so that we can work together to create a more just and equitable society.

The bishops' clear statement that racism is a life issue is extremely important today as the Church looks for ways to make the case in the public forum for respecting all human life, including the unborn and the victims of racism. The consistent ethic of life proposed by the American bishops gains credibility when it includes attention to the victims of racism.

Part II

MEDITATIONS ON CATHOLIC SOCIAL TEACHING

Despite significant progress, Catholic Social Teaching (CST) is still too unknown. In 2023, Loyola University in New Orleans conducted a survey of Catholics involved in social ministry. The survey found that 90 percent knew something about CST but did not have a firm grasp of its themes and positions. Furthermore, most of the respondents thought that their diocese was cutting back on CST programing, that their parishes put too little emphasis on preaching and practices of CST, and that their fellow Catholics knew little or nothing about CST. This revealing study reminds us that much more must be done at all levels to spread this important message.

The following meditations are designed to engage the reader in personal reflection on specific moral issues in the light of CST principles. Since the moral issues are complex and often controversial, I have approached each one from diverse perspectives. All the meditations provide relevant background material on the issue and specific elements of CST, as well as a question to guide reflection on their interaction. Some of the meditations present a balanced view of the topic, while others treat just one side that encourages the reader to look for subsequent meditations that deal with the other side. Some make use of secular arguments, while others stay within a religious framework. Some repeat large segments from previous chapters, while others offer fresh material. Some contain a set prayer, while others leave room for various prayerful responses.

Practically, there are numerous ways the meditations can be effectively used. Individuals can meditate on one that deals with a personally troubling issue. Families can use them as a basis for discussion and action during Advent and Lent. Social Justice Committees can use them to create a reflective atmosphere before their regular meetings. Priests and deacons can use them in preparing their homilies on social concerns. The more individuals and groups appropriate CST, the better chance that parishes will incorporate the tradition in their worship and mission— which, as we have seen, is the most effective vehicle for revealing more of this valuable treasure.

4

EUTHANASIA

Diverse Perspectives

Over the last few decades, there has been a growing discussion of the ethics of euthanasia (physicians administering lethal drugs) and assisted suicide (physicians making lethal drugs available). In the vast literature supporting some form of assisted death, there are common themes. It is a way for dying patients to choose death over a life filled with physical and emotional suffering. Human beings have a right to determine how they live their lives, including how and when they die, and others should respect this right. Physicians should have compassion for their suffering patients: they should not abandon them as they approach death, but should assist them in their desire to die. Since it is ethically legitimate to remove dying patients from a life support machine causing death (passive euthanasia), providing drugs (active euthanasia) to accomplish the same goal should also be ethically legitimate. Hastening death can be an act of charity toward loved ones so their burdens of care and financial support are reduced or limited. Controlling the time of death can provide time for goodbyes to loved ones and can facilitate the donation of organs.

Over the last century, Catholic Social Teaching has gradually developed a more sophisticated position against euthanasia, culminating in the 2020 Vatican letter on end-of-life issues, appropriately titled *Samaritanus bonus* ("The Good Samaritan"). It reaffirms the Church's traditional opposition to euthanasia as a "crime against humanity," "a grave violation of the Law of God," and "an intrinsically evil act." It is important to note that the letter immediately adds that individuals suffering from "anguish and despair" may make an error of judgment and in good faith request euthanasia without any personal guilt. It goes on to base its definitive prohibition of assisted dying on the natural law, known by reason and on God's commandment, "Thou shall not kill." Furthermore, Christ's command to love our neighbor, exemplified in the parable of the good Samaritan, prompts us to practice an "ethic of care" for the dying by accompanying them on the final part of their earthly journey and by casting on them a "contemplative gaze" that recognizes their essential dignity and fragile vulnerability. As Christians who believe earthly death is a passage to eternal life, we have an obligation to do our part to support the dying with care and love so that they can persevere in the final, definitive, free act of surrendering totally to the living God.

The Vatican letter explicitly rejects various arguments that assisted death is a legitimate response to human suffering. For instance, it fails to recognize that human life is "a value in itself." As Christians, we recall that Jesus Christ freely accepted the horrible physical and emotional suffering of death on the cross and that God raised him to a new glorified life. For believers, this means unavoidable suffering of all types can be meaningful and redemptive, when endured with hope and trust in God.

It also rejects the claim that euthanasia is a legitimate compassionate response to the suffering of terminally ill patients, insisting that true compassion "consists not in causing death, but in embracing the sick" and "offering them affection, attention, and the means to alleviate their suffering."

The letter identifies questionable cultural trends that support assisted death, including an individualism that emphasizes personal fulfillment over serving the common good, and freedom from constraints over cultivating mutual relationships. A culture that celebrates such individualism often leaves a dying person without the warm personal love and support needed as death approaches. CST teaches that we are social creatures who find fulfillment in loving relationships with persons who can be good Samaritans for us on the final stages of our earthly journey.

Question: Does CST support or challenge my personal outlook on euthanasia?

Prolonging Life

The Catholic moral tradition and its articulation in modern Catholic Social Teaching not only forbids euthanasia (death through a lethal drug administered by a physician), but it also excludes, in some cases, aggressive medical treatment. The secular discussion of the ethics of prolonging life tends toward two extremes: doing everything possible by any means to extend life, and having no ethical obligation to do anything.

Taking a more nuanced approach, the American Medical Association (AMA) has developed guidelines for a physician caring for terminally ill patients. Physicians have the twofold commitment to sustain life and to relive suffering. When the two are in conflict, the preferences of the patient should prevail. "The principle of patient autonomy" requires physicians to respect the decision of competent patients to forgo life-sustaining treatments that do not reverse the underlying medical condition such as mechanical ventilation, renal dialysis, and artificial nutrition and hydration. In this regard, the guidelines clearly state that "there is no ethical distinction between withdrawing and withholding life-sustaining treatment." Promoting the "dignity and autonomy of dying patients" also includes "providing effective palliative treatment even though it may foreseeably hasten death."

Chapter 5 of the Vatican letter, "The Good Samaritan," takes up the issue of extending life in the second section, entitled "The moral obligation to exclude aggressive medical treatment." It begins with a general principle: "The dignity of the human person entails the right to die with the greatest possible serenity and with one's proper human and Christian dignity intact." The letter recognizes that modern medicine can "artificially delay death, often without real benefit to the patient." When death is imminent, it is "lawful according to science and conscience to renounce treatments that provide only a precarious and painful extension of life."

The renunciation of "extraordinary" or "disproportionate" means is not equivalent to suicide or euthanasia, it rather expresses an acceptance of the limitations of the human condition and respect for the wishes of dying patients. As to removing artificial means of nourishment and hydration from the terminally ill, the Vatican document states: "When the provision of nutrition and hydration no longer benefits the patient," or "causes harm or intolerable suffering," their "administration should be suspended." This "does not unlawfully hasten death," but "respects the natural course of the critical and terminal illness."

In sum, human beings have a right to nutrition and hydration, and artificial means, such as a feeding tube, can help meet that need. It is morally legitimate both to refuse such extraordinary artificial means to prolong life and to remove them when they do more harm than good. From a Christian perspective, all care for dying persons should be guided by the example of the Good Samaritan, who prompts us to accompany them on their journey to God with respect and compassion.

Question: What part of CST on prolonging life is most helpful to me? What part is most challenging?

Cost Containment

There is a growing worldwide movement to legalize physician-assisted dying. At least nineteen countries allow it, making the practice available to some 200 million individuals. In the United States, the Supreme Court decided, in 1967, that the Constitution does not protect the right of competent, terminally ill patients to commit suicide with the assistance of a physician, effectively leaving it up to each state to decide the legality of physician-assisted dying. In 1994 Oregon passed the "Death With Dignity Act," which allows terminally ill residents of the state to end their lives through the voluntary self-administration of a lethal dose of a medication expressly prescribed by a physician for that purpose. By 2022, nine other states had legalized physician-assisted suicide, including California and New Jersey. Thirty-three states have laws explicitly prohibiting assisted dying, including Ohio and Michigan.

In the United States, advocates of legalization note that a well-timed decision to end life could save a lot of money for both federally funded programs and private purchasers of health care. Hemlock Society founder Derek Humphry calls cost containment the "unspoken argument" for the legalization of assisted suicide.

In an article on "Dying Well, Assisted Suicide, and the Law," Cathleen Kaveny, one of our best commentators on Catholic Social Teaching, argues against legalizing physician-assisted dying. She begins by insisting that there are "solid nonsectarian reasons" against legalization. To support her case, she cites a 1994 New York State Task Force on Life and the Law that unanimously concluded that legalization would be profoundly dangerous for large segments of the population, especially poor and marginalized persons.

Kaveny, who has degrees in law and theology, sees legalization of suicide as a slippery slope gradually expanding options and incentives for early death. She imagines physicians subtly encouraging terminally ill patients to choose a painless legal way to end their lives. Legalization of assisted suicide could easily lead to legalizing euthanasia that involves a physician administering a lethal drug. The right to die granted to terminally ill patients could easily be expanded to chronically ill persons. The right of competent persons to choose assisted suicide could logically be extended to surrogate decision makers on behalf of noncompetent patients who are suffering. For Kaveny, the slippery slope is steep and dangerous to the common good.

The cost containment argument for legalization has gained momentum in the last decade as the cost of care for terminally ill patients has risen, constituting as much as 10 percent of the nation's health care expenditures. In this situation, dying patients may feel a duty or responsibility to end their life quickly. Recognizing the challenge posed by rising health costs, Kaveny insists that multiplying assisted suicides is not a wise or moral solution. Such a policy denies the fundamental dignity of all human beings and erodes our capacity to assist those who most need our care. Furthermore, it fails to recognize that dying can be an important life experience for the terminally ill person and for their loved ones. Our real task as a society is to act with justice and charity so that everyone has access to basic health care, which always includes comfort care and pain control for terminally ill persons. As Pope Francis has expressed it, "We are called to accompany people toward death. But not provoke death or facilitate assisted suicide. Indeed life is a right, not death, which must be welcomed, not administered."[1]

Question: How do I view using euthanasia for cost containment?

Unbearable Suffering

The issues of euthanasia are complex and emotionally charged. In the United States, where each state can decide about legalizing assisted suicide, some forty state legislatures have resisted strong pressure to provide their citizens with that option. One of the strongest and most emotional arguments for legislation is the unbearable suffering experienced by some seriously ill and dying patients. For example, a retired family doctor shares the story of his twenty-five-year-old mentally competent daughter who was blind and suffered intensely from a seventeen-year battle with leukemia. At one point, she asked him to give her enough sleeping pills so she would go to sleep permanently. He did not do so because at that time it was not legal anywhere in the United States. Reflecting on the experience, he now says that, with a legal option, he would have given her a lethal dose as an act of love and compassion. Such poignant stories multiplied many times over—some familiar and personal—form a highly emotional argument for legalizing assisted suicide.

Christianity, which celebrates the passion, death, and resurrection of Jesus Christ as the key event in all human history, provides us with a distinctive perspective on human suffering. We are persons with infinite longings and finite capabilities who cannot avoid emotional, mental, and spiritual suffering. We are inspirited bodies and embodied spirits who are subject to physical pain, debilitating illness, and the diminishments of disease and age. As theists, we believe in a God of compassion and mercy who is on our side in the great struggle against suffering and evil. As Christians, we believe in Jesus Christ, who transformed suffering, conquered death, and opened the possibility of salvation for all people. Faithful persons in our tradition talk about joining their sufferings with the crucified Christ and of befriending death as a passage to eternal life with the risen Christ. Others say they offer their sufferings each day for a specific person or cause.

Although modern medicine and hospice care have done wonders to alleviate and manage the suffering of so many dying persons, we are still faced with the stark fact of unrelieved, unbearable suffering of fellow members of the human family. We can imagine some possible responses: admiring the heroic persons who persevere to the end; being grateful for those who offer their suffering as part of their care and prayer for others; having compassion for those overwhelmed by pain who choose suicide while entrusting them to the gracious God, who is infinitely merciful and all-loving; praying for suffering patients and compassionate physicians faced with immense suffering and heart wrenching decisions; avoiding glib talk and easy answers to perplexing and profound questions about intense human suffering; asking God for the courage and strength to accept our own unavoidable sufferings whatever they may be. In some circumstances, it seems wise to maintain a reverent, humble, prayerful silence before the mystery of evil in the form of intense human suffering.

Question: What are my thoughts and feelings about euthanasia as a solution to unbearable suffering?

5

ABORTION

Traditional Teaching

Let us begin with a brief history of traditional Catholic teaching on the objective morality of the act of abortion, which terminates fetal life. There is no clear explicit biblical teaching on this issue. The Hebrew Scriptures speak tenderly of God forming each new life in the womb (cf. Jer 1:5) but say nothing about the morality of abortion. In the Gospels, Jesus explicitly forbids some practices, such as divorce, but does not include abortion. In his epistles, the Apostle Paul consistently condemns sexual immorality but does not mention abortion.

The earliest Christian condemnations of abortion are found in first-century documents. For example, the *Didache*, probably written near the end of the first century, clearly states: "You shall not procure [an] abortion, nor destroy a newborn child" (*Didache* 2:1–2), a procedure widely practiced in the pagan world. A document written about the same time known as the *Epistle of Barnabas* condemns abortion as a violation of Christ's command to love our neighbor.[1] By the fifth century, Augustine, representing a growing consensus in the Christian East and West, condemned abortion at all stages of fetal development. In the thirteenth century, Aquinas, who thought that a fetus only gradually acquired a human soul, still taught that abortion at all stages of fetal development is "a grave sin against the natural law," and after ensoulment at forty days is a "graver sin of homicide."

By the sixteenth century, there was still a solid Christian witness against abortion. The reformers Martin Luther and John Calvin both condemned abortion, even though they found no explicit biblical prohibition of it. Calvin, for example, taught that the fetus "enclosed in the womb of its mother, is already a human being, and it is a monstrous crime to rob it of the life which it has not yet begun to enjoy."[2]

In an 1864 encyclical, Pope Pius IX attached excommunication to the crime of "direct abortion" from the moment of conception, but he did justify "indirect abortion" when saving the life of the mother would involve the death of the fetus, as in the case of removing a cancerous pregnant uterus.

In his 1996 encyclical, *The Gospel of Life*, Pope John Paul II echoed Vatican II in condemning abortion as an "unspeakable crime," and added a pastoral word to women who have had an abortion, reminding them that the Father of mercies offers them forgiveness and peace. Pope Francis has frequently reaffirmed the traditional teaching of the Church, calling abortion "a crime," "an absolute evil," and even "murder." At the same time, Francis has expressed compassion for women who procured an abortion under extreme pressure of an "existential and moral ordeal," which made them feel it was their only option.

This brief selective history provides strong support for the Church's long and consistent opposition to abortion. It also invites further reflection on the moral and pastoral implications of the shift from the primitive Aristotelian biology to modern embryology.

Questions: What is my personal reaction to this traditional teaching?

When Does Human Life Begin?

Throughout Christian history, theologians have wrestled with the question of when the fetus becomes a human being. The early fathers of the Church typically distinguished an unformed fetus from one that is more fully formed, assigning greater blame to aborting a more developed fetus. For example, St. Basil the Great (d. 391) condemned abortion at all stages of development, but called aborting a formed fetus "premeditated murder."

Influenced by the philosophy and the biology of Aristotle, Thomas Aquinas (d. 1274) taught that the developing fetus is successively animated by a vegetative soul, an animal soul, and finally a human soul, in a process called "ensoulment." This theory had a certain plausibility given the prevailing understanding of the reproductive process that the male sperm was, in potential, a new human being, and that this development occurred in the female uterus. It was not until the 1870s that a scientific consensus emerged that babies were produced by joining the male sperm with the female egg or ovum. This process produced a new tiny single cell entity called a "zygote" that travels from one of the two fallopian tubes to the uterus and implants itself in the lining of the uterus in a process called "implantation."

These discoveries of reproductive biology have moved Catholic theologians to question whether an individual human life is present immediately after fertilization. For example, Karl Rahner asserts that the claim that a fetus from the first moment of conception is a human being can no longer "be held with certainty and is open to positive doubt." Richard McCormick describes the embryo during the first two weeks as "nascent human life" that then develops later into an "individual human life." Charles Curran notes that, during the first two weeks of pregnancy, a zygote can split into two viable embryos in a process called "twinning," which raises a "speculative doubt" about the humanity of the zygote at this stage of development, although, in practice, it should be treated as having a human soul. It is important to note that all of these influential theologians have consistently supported the Church teaching that abortion is intrinsically evil and morally wrong.

In a June 2021 *New York Times* op-ed, provocatively titled "The American Bishops Are Wrong about Biden and Abortion,"[3] the Catholic historian Garry Wills includes a critique of the bishops' teaching that fetal life is human life from the moment of conception. In what might be considered an extension of the Thomistic ensoulment argument, Wills makes the following points: neither Augustine nor Aquinas were sure when fetal life acquired a human soul; most fertilized ova are spontaneously aborted; the Church does not baptize miscarriages; and polls show most Catholics do not accept the teaching of their bishops that human life begins at conception.

In response to the Wills op-ed, the *National Review* published an article, "Garry Wills Is Wrong about the Bishops and Abortion,"[4] which claims he "grotesquely manipulates the facts," offers a "sloppy defense of abortion," employs "sophomoric arguments," and distorts the views of Augustine and Aquinas.

Whatever merits of these broad criticisms, Garry Wills has contributed to the public debate on abortion by drawing the attention of a wide audience to the important ongoing discussion within the Catholic community on ensoulment and when human life first begins in the reproductive process.

Question: Does the scientific knowledge of fetal development influence my view on the morality of abortion?

Strategies of the American Bishops

Before the 1960s, the American bishops said very little in opposition to abortion. They concentrated instead on social issues that were important to the growing number of Catholic immigrants. For example, in the late nineteenth century, they supported the establishment of labor unions, and in 1919 they published a "Program of Social Reconstruction" that called for various social reforms, including laws restricting child labor, equal pay for women, and a mandated minimum wage.

In his book *The Social Mission of the U.S. Catholic Church*, theologian Charles Curran recounts the history of how the American bishops have come to make abortion their major focus, spending "more time, energy and money" on it than any other single issue. Soon after the 1973 Supreme Court *Roe v. Wade* decision, the bishops adopted a threefold plan: to convince the faithful that abortion is wrong; to assist pregnant women; and to pass a constitutional amendment protecting fetal life. Before the 1976 presidential election, the bishops issued a statement declaring they did not want to form a voting bloc or tell Catholics how to vote and urging the faithful to consider the position of candidates on a full range of issues without giving priority to abortion or any other single issue.

In the 1980s, Cardinal Joseph Bernardin advocated framing opposition to abortion in the context of a "consistent ethic of life" that opposes war, capital punishment, and other threats to life. In the 1990s, the bishops began to speak of abortion as the fundamental human rights issue of our day, because it attacks life itself, the most fundamental of human goods. In the 2015 voter guide, "Forming Conscience for Faithful Citizenship," the United States Conference of Catholic Bishops (USCCB) called abortion a "preeminent threat" to human dignity.

Not all the bishops have supported the growing use of the word "preeminent" to distinguish abortion from other life issues. As a prime example, Cardinal Robert McElroy of San Diego, who has doctorates in theology and political science, notes that the word does not appear in the official *Compendium of Catholic Social Teaching* and insists that it has unavoidable political connotations in the context of U.S. polarized partisanship. The cardinal argues that Catholic Social Teaching deals with many social issues that are united by a shared concern to serve the common good, and that making abortion preeminent reduces the common good to a single issue. He emphasizes that climate change is a more foundational issue than abortion since it threatens to end the whole human race. In an interview, McElroy agreed that abortion is "a preeminent issue for Catholics" and then added "one of several." In this regard, it is helpful to recall that official Church documents have taken a broader approach, for example, teaching that both abortion and racism are intrinsic evils.

This line of thought suggests that the case against abortion can be expressed not in terms of its unique depravity but as an integral part of a consistent ethic of life that promotes the common good. McElroy has also argued that calling abortion the preeminent issue is "at least discordant if not inconsistent" with the teachings of Pope Francis, who advises against "obsessing over abortion" and favors a less confrontational and more dialogic approach to public conversations.[5] In essence, Cardinal McElroy contends that an inclusive approach to the abortion issue is more faithful to modern Catholic Social Teaching and has a better chance of gaining the support of the Catholic community and the public at large.

Question: Which approach seems best to me?

Women Sharing Their Stories

In the Catholic community where an all-male celibate clergy makes official pronouncements regarding abortion, it is especially important to hear the stories of women who procure abortions and who carry pregnancies to full term. Let us consider four typical stories.

In a November 2022 *Commonweal* article called "This Pregnancy," the Catholic writer Mary Gordon, now in her early eighties, shares a personal experience from when she was nineteen, a student on scholarship at Barnard College in New York City, living with her widowed mother.[6] She missed a period, thought it was not possible that she was pregnant, and consulted a gynecologist, who confirmed that she was ten weeks pregnant and told her that for two thousand dollars he could get a psychiatrist to write a letter saying she was suicidal so she could get a legal abortion. Lacking the money, she arranged for an illegal abortion that involved a blindfolded car ride though the Bronx to an unknown destination, where a man who did not speak English gave her a pain killer and performed the "excruciating" procedure. That night, Mary stayed with a friend who comforted her as she wept from the memory of the pain and the awareness that she could have died.

In her 1982 book, *In a Different Voice*, Harvard researcher Carol Gilligan records the thought process of Janet, a twenty-four-year-old married Catholic, pregnant again two months after the birth of her first child.[7] She believes abortion is taking a human life, even if the fetus is only potentially human, but she is not ready right now to be tied down with two children. She wonders if getting an abortion would be selfish on her part, but she also has to think of what is best for her son and her husband. She asks herself if she should be so morally strict as to hurt her loving husband. Perhaps, she thinks, an abortion would be a form of self-sacrifice for her own good and the good of her family. Finally, Janet concludes her anguished ruminations by expressing her belief that "God can punish, but He can also forgive."

A parishioner, who for privacy we will call Lydia, wants to tell her story to help other women who are feeling guilty about having an abortion:

> I have been very blessed in my life with a loving family, a good education, a rewarding career, a marvelous marriage partner and a beautiful two-year-old daughter. Suddenly I was no longer interested in being intimate with my husband, who fortunately was willing to be patient with me. I consulted my parish priest, who listened patiently to me for several sessions, until one time I unexpectedly blurted out that I had an abortion before I met my husband and that I had never told him and am feeling very guilty and reluctant to tell him now. My pastor then suggested I concentrate on accepting God's

forgiveness. We met weekly to reflect together on God's unconditional love and on Gospel stories of divine mercy, especially the parable of the prodigal son. A little over a month into our weekly sessions, I decided to go to confession and felt great relief in celebrating the sacrament of God's pardon and peace. A few weeks later, I called my pastor and told him I didn't need to see him anymore, because I am now able once again to participate fully in our marital intimacy.

Fifteen years ago, in my second year of grad school, I got pregnant and my boyfriend, supported by my parents, urged me to get an abortion, which I found morally repugnant. Desperate, I sought help from an organization called EMPA (Emotional and Material Pregnancy Aid). With their help, I was able to give birth to a beautiful daughter, to raise her as a single mom, and eventually complete my graduate studies. Today, I am happily married with a second daughter and a good job that I can do from home. I am especially grateful to the EMPA volunteer who was constantly there for me through the entire time with encouragement, good advice, and help in getting financial assistance and scholarship money.

By being more attentive to the real-life experiences of women, the Catholic Church will be a more effective and credible participant in the ongoing search for workable state policies on abortion.

Question: What is my emotional reaction to these stories?

Rules for Discussion

In his 1981 book *How Brave a New World*, the highly respected Jesuit moral theologian Richard McCormick presented "Rules for Abortion Debate" as a response to the 1973 Supreme Court *Roe v. Wade* decision legalizing abortion.[8] Some of his rules seem even more significant now after the 2022 *Dobbs v. Jackson Women's Health Organization* decision overturned *Roe*, leaving policy decisions to individual states.

- Attempt to identify areas of agreement. In this regard, recent polls show 85 percent of Americans agree abortion should be legal at least in some circumstances and 90 percent agree that abortion should not be legal after viability. State legislatures could start to construct workable policies on abortion around fundamental agreements like these.
- Avoid using slogans. McCormick gives two examples that are still relevant today. The first is calling abortion "murder" (a slogan that Pope Francis himself used in a recent informal interview). McCormick argues that the word *murder* is a "composite value term" that means morally unjustified killing of another person. Calling abortion murder involves a disputed assumption that human life begins at conception. Furthermore, it is totally unnecessary to use that slogan to defend the Church's opposition to abortion. The other slogan is that "a woman has a right to her own body," even more commonly used today. This slogan has several questionable assumptions: for example, that the fetus is simply part of a woman's body, and that her bodily rights are absolute. Slogans tend to harden entrenched positions; they do not further dialogue or compromise.
- Distinguish morality and public policy. With the *Dobbs* decision, this distinction takes on added significance. For example, it is possible to view abortion as morally wrong but at the same time to recognize that a total legal prohibition of abortion is not a wise or workable policy in a country so passionately polarized on this issue. Pro-life advocates should not let the perfect be the enemy of the good.
- Try to identify the core issue at stake. In our post-*Dobbs* world, the real task is to develop public policies and pass state laws that will allow our diverse society to live in relative peace and harmony. Unfortunately, so far many states have used the new opportunity not to seek consensus or make compromises but to pass extreme legislation. For

example, some states have outlawed all abortions, while others encourage total abortion access without some reasonable restrictions that could gain greater public support.

- Distinguish morality and pastoral care. In practice today, this could encourage pro-life advocates who worked hard to overturn *Roe* to put forth a similar effort to find ways to support pregnant women and new mothers. This might mean accompanying a pregnant unsupported teenager through her pregnancy and after giving birth. It could also mean advocating for greater public assistance for single mothers. Workable public policies have to consider the rights of both fetal life and pregnant women.

- Distinguish the pairs: right-wrong and good-bad. Catholic theology holds that abortion is objectively wrong and never right. It also recognizes that circumstances and intentions can make a personal decision for abortion subjectively good and not bad, as when a person sincerely follows an erroneous conscience. This distinction can facilitate dialogue. For example, a pro-life advocate can view his pro-choice friend as a good person with good intentions, who has made a wrong judgment on the morality of abortion. This sets a framework for continued friendship and honest dialogue.

Question: Which of these rules is most helpful to me in discussing abortion?

Positive Responses to the *Dobbs* Decision

On June 24, 2022, the Supreme Court issued a historic decision in the *Dobbs v. Jackson Women's Health Organization* case that has altered the entire approach to abortion in the United States. By a 5 to 4 majority, the Court overturned the 1973 *Roe* ruling that the Constitution grants the right to abortion, and by a 6 to 3 margin upheld the right of individual states to make laws regulating abortion. Writing for the majority, Justice Samuel Alito defended overturning such a long-established law on the grounds that the *Roe* constitutional argument is "egregiously wrong" and is not "deeply rooted in the nation's history and tradition."

Let us consider some positive responses to the *Dobbs* decision. The USCCB, which for almost fifty years made overturning *Roe* their major public policy objective, lauded the decision as "historic in the life of our country," overturning an unjust law that "legalized and normalized" the taking of innocent human lives and resulted in the "deaths of millions of preborn children."[9] The statement praised the countless ordinary Americans who supported the pro-life cause, one of the "great movements for social change and civil rights in our nation's history." The USCCB statement concluded with a call for "reasoned reflection and civil dialogue" to heal our wounds and create a more just society, where "every pregnant woman has the needed resources to bring her child into the world in love."

Looking ahead to the post-*Dobbs* era, twenty pro-life scholars, including papal biographer George Weigel and Princeton professor of jurisprudence Robert George, published a statement, "Protecting the Unborn," which offers guidance for the ongoing discussion of state laws on abortion. A just pro-life society would meet the "myriad needs of pregnant women," the statement said, while legally protecting unborn children at every stage of development. Since our political realities make full protection of the unborn impossible, it is morally justified to support the best law possible. The scholars recall the traditional axiom: "The perfect should not be the enemy of the good."

It can be morally appropriate to support laws that ban some or most elective abortions even though they permit abortion in the case of "rape or incest or fetal abnormality, or at some early stages of pregnancy." The scholars justify this practice with the reminder that "law making is the art of the possible."

David Cloutier, who teaches theology at Catholic University, welcomed the *Dobbs* decision that transfers the responsibility for solving our abortion disputes from the courts to state legislatures, where the democratic process can lead to effective solutions. He recognizes that "moral zealotry" can sabotage this process, but he still hopes that states will make bipartisan attempts to find solutions that serve the common good. Furthermore, he believes states can serve as valuable social laboratories for forging an "alternative social framework" that meets the needs of pregnant girls and women. Some Catholic theologians noted that *Dobbs* opened up the possibility for states to serve as valuable social laboratories for forging creative responses to the abortion issue.

Question: What do I make of these affirmative responses to the Dobbs *decision?*

Negative Responses to the *Dobbs* Decision

The 2022 Supreme Court decision that overturned *Roe* and granted individual states the right to legislate on abortion won the support of the Catholic bishops and a large majority of white evangelical leaders, but it has also generated widespread opposition. In their joint dissent, Justices Breyer, Sotomayor, and Kagan argued that the majority "decimated women's reproductive freedom," and "undermined a woman's personal autonomy." This decision opened the possibility of restrictive state laws banning all abortions from conception and even prosecuting women who seek abortions. The dissenters worry that the Court will now overturn other established rights, such as same-sex marriage. Furthermore, they accuse the majority of undermining the traditional image of the Supreme Court as a stable institution, since a simple change in the membership of the Court overturned a long-established right.

Echoing the Court minority and typifying many women's organizations, the League of Women Voters issued a statement claiming that *Dobbs* deprives women of their "bodily autonomy," which means they are "no longer equal individuals in our democracy." Furthermore, it will exacerbate societal inequities, disproportionately impacting women of color and low-income communities. The League concluded its statement: "We will use our anger to fight in the legislatures, the courts and the streets."

In the November 2022 issue of *Commonweal*, Cathleen Kaveny, who teaches law and theology at Boston College, published a response to *Dobbs* that criticizes both the majority and minority opinions while proposing a third way forward.[10] She points out that the 1973 *Roe* decision produced "a raging political controversy" about abortion, which has gotten more polarized over the years and today divides the country along partisan lines. For example, in 2022 70 percent of Republicans identify as pro-life, as do only 10 percent of Democrats. Kaveny sees *Dobbs* as a "radical decision" which will exacerbate the culture wars, with conservative states restricting abortion and progressive states becoming "sanctuaries" for pregnant women. At the same time, Kaveny criticizes the Court minority for not recognizing the failure of *Roe* to end the national acrimonious debate over abortion.

Searching for a viable alternative, Professor Kaveny lauds Chief Justice Roberts for upholding the Mississippi law banning almost all abortions after fifteen weeks as "not unduly burdensome," but refusing to join the majority in overturning *Roe*. She sees Roberts's position as a "possible blueprint" for a workable compromise which would allow abortions before fifteen weeks but ban them after that.

Recent polls suggest Americans would support this type of compromise. For example, substantial majorities agree that abortion should be legal in at least some or all circumstances but should not be allowed after viability, unless the health of the mother is at stake. At this time, it is hard to imagine state legislatures actually working in a bipartisan way to pass legislation that reflects this public consensus. Nevertheless, the Christian virtue of hope encourages us to avoid a paralyzing pessimism and to continue our efforts to find common ground, trusting that God will not let any of our good endeavors be lost or wasted.

Question: What aspect of the dissent is most significant to me?

Bishops Denying Communion

On the inauguration of Joseph R. Biden as the forty-sixth president of the United States, Archbishop Gomez, the president of the United States Conference of Catholic Bishops (USCCB), issued a statement praising Biden for his personal piety and longstanding commitment to the poor, but criticizing him for policies that threaten human life—especially abortion, the "preeminent priority" of the USCCB.[11] This criticism of Biden signaled the desire of some bishops to deny communion to Catholic politicians who support legal abortion.

This is not the first time Joe Biden has faced this threat. In 2008, Joseph Bambera, bishop of Scranton, Pennsylvania, declared that Joe Biden running for vice president on the Obama ticket could not receive communion in his diocese because of his support for legalized abortion. During the 2020 campaign, Fr. Robert Morey, the pastor of St. Anthony Catholic Church in Florence, South Carolina, very publicly refused to give Biden communion when he came forward to receive, saying that "any public figure who advocates for abortion places himself or herself outside of Church teaching."[12] Later, Morey explained that "Holy Communion signifies we are one with God, each other and the Church," and that he had a moral responsibility to be a faithful minister of the Church, "even in the most difficult situations," adding that he would pray for Mr. Biden.

After President Biden's inauguration, some Catholic bishops publicly argued that he should not be allowed to receive communion. Retired Archbishop Charles Chaput insisted that Catholics like Biden who go to communion "give scandal to the faithful" by creating the impression that the moral laws of the Church are optional. Furthermore, bishops who are willing to allow Biden to receive communion "do a disservice to their brother bishops and their people."[13] Archbishop Joseph Naumann of Kansas City said Biden should stop "defining himself as a devout Catholic" and should refrain from presenting himself for communion at Mass.

After the USCCB decided not to adopt a national policy forbidding communion to any public officials, individual bishops took the initiative to restrict communion to certain individuals in their own diocese. In May 2022, Archbishop Salvatore Cordileone said that then–House Speaker Nancy Pelosi could no longer receive communion in his diocese because she continued to support legal abortion. In a public letter, the archbishop said that after numerous attempts to talk to Pelosi about "the grave evil she is perpetrating, the scandal she is causing, and the danger to her own soul she is risking," he decided to ban her from communion in his diocese.[14]

Pelosi, who considers herself a "devout Catholic" and regularly goes to Mass, said not being able to receive communion would be a "severe blow." She continues to receive communion in Washington and in June 2022 received communion at a papal mass in the Vatican. While the restrictive approach of Archbishop Cordileone and a few others have generated media attention, most U.S. bishops have quietly avoided direct confrontations and public rebukes.

Question: What is my opinion on denying communion to Catholic politicians who are personally opposed to abortion but think it should be legal?

Weaponizing the Eucharist

Some American bishops have pushed back against their colleagues who have publicly criticized President Biden and restricted his access to receive communion. After Archbishop Gomez criticized Biden for pursuing policies that threaten human life, especially legalizing abortion, Cardinal Blasé Cupich of Chicago said the criticism of Biden was "ill-considered," unprecedented, and was not endorsed by the whole conference of bishops. Cardinal Joseph Tobin of Newark noted that excluding Catholic leaders from communion would "thrust the bishops of our nation into the very heart of the toxic partisan strife which has distorted our political culture and crippled meaningful dialogue."[15]

The most persuasive arguments for not denying communion to Catholic public figures have come from Cardinal Robert McElroy of San Diego. Echoing Pope Francis, he calls for "dialogue, not judgment; collaboration, not isolation; truth in charity, not harshness."[16] McElroy insists that we need a "pathway of reconciliation" that places the "healing of our society ahead of any specific policy issue." For him, "repairing the soul of our country is the pre-requisite for any sustainable effort to advance the common good."[17] Following the example of Pope Francis, we should "reach out to President Biden in his humanity, a man of Catholic faith striving to serve his nation and his God." The cardinal warns against "weaponizing" the Eucharist, citing the pope's statement that the Eucharist is not "a prize for the perfect but a powerful medicine and nourishment for the weak" (*Evangelii gaudium* no. 47).

Commenting on the well-publicized debate among the bishops, McElroy said it already had a "tremendously damaging impact" by thrusting the toxic political culture into the life of the Church and the Catholic community. He went on to warn that denying communion to Biden or some other prominent Catholic would do even greater damage to the unity of the Church and popular understanding of the Eucharist.

McElroy claims that some bishops not only have made abortion the preeminent moral issue of our time but also "a de facto litmus test for determining whether a Catholic public official is a faithful Catholic,"[18] a stance that reduces the common good to a single issue.

President Biden has a lot of support in his desire to participate fully in Mass every Sunday. In a personal meeting with Pope Francis, Biden said that the pope told him he is welcome to receive communion. Cardinal Wilton Gregory, Archbishop of Washington, DC, said he seeks common ground with the president and welcomes him to receive communion in his diocese, where Biden regularly attends Sunday Mass at Holy Trinity Church. Likewise, various bishops of Wilmington, Delaware, have allowed Biden to receive communion in his home parish, St. Joseph on the Brandywine, where he typically arrives slightly late for Mass, sits in the back of church, receives communion, and leaves before the crowd. Most American bishops have followed the broad approach of Pope Francis, who urges the clergy to be shepherds who exercise compassion and not politicians who issue condemnations.

Question: What is my opinion of weaponizing the Eucharist?

Electoral Politics

When John F. Kennedy, a Catholic senator from Massachusetts, ran for president in 1960, abortion was not a major issue. He won 78 percent of the Catholic vote, helping him defeat Richard Nixon and become the first Catholic president of the United States. In 2002, John F. Kerry, another Catholic senator from Massachusetts with the initials JFK, ran for president when abortion had become a major issue—in fact, the decisive issue for many Catholics. Bishop Raymond Burke of St. Louis publicly announced that Kerry could not receive communion in his diocese. A strong "Catholics against Kerry" movement developed in Ohio, which became the key battleground state. The Kerry campaign found it hard to find parishes in northwest Ohio where the candidate was welcome to attend Sunday Mass and receive communion. John F. Kerry lost 52 percent of the Catholic vote, lost Ohio by a narrow margin, and lost the presidency to George W. Bush.

In 2020, when Joe Biden, a practicing Catholic, sought the White House, abortion was once again a major issue. Some bishops made public statements declaring that Catholics could not vote for candidates who support abortion, the preeminent moral evil of our time, an implicit but clear signal to Catholics not to vote for Biden. Nevertheless, he did win almost half of the Catholic vote and became the second Catholic president in U.S. history.

The Supreme Court *Dobbs* decision on June 24, 2022, which overturned *Roe*, has transferred the focus of abortion politics to the state level. It is complicated, but some commentators argue that the *Dobbs* decision played a role in the 2022 midterm elections, limiting Democratic losses in the House and enabling them to retain the Senate. We do know that five statewide ballot measures favoring abortion rights won, including the red states of Kentucky and Montana. Some governors who favor restricting abortion, however, won easily, such as Ron DeSantis in Florida and Greg Abbott in Texas.

Since *Dobbs*, states have so far tended to adopt extreme public policies. California, for example, has passed laws making abortion medications readily available to students at state universities and helping to pay for pregnant women traveling to the state to obtain an abortion. At the other extreme, Alabama has a near total ban on abortion, as do eleven other states with the common exemption of preserving the life of the mother. So far, the hope that *Dobbs* would prompt reasoned debate and workable compromises in individual states has not materialized, in large part because of the polarized partisan politics that dominate any discussion of abortion.

In this polarized situation, Catholic Social Teaching calls us to do whatever we can to find just policies that serve the common good. That might look like having a long delayed, often feared conversation with a friend or relative on abortion; concentrating on state policies and not the morality of abortion; seeking to understand and not persuade; bracketing the labels *pro-life* and *pro-choice*; and searching for common ground. We could also pay more attention to candidates for state offices, considering their character, competence, and policy positions, including their willingness to seek common ground on abortion. As Christians, we can all pray that God guides and blesses our various efforts to find just, workable solutions to our seemingly intractable impasse on abortion policy.

Question: How can I help promote just and effective state abortion policies?

6

CARING FOR CREATION

The Threat of Air Pollution

The United Nations Environment Programme (UNEP) views pollution as a major threat to the earth and its inhabitants. UNEP reports that air pollution is the largest cause of disease and premature death in the world, with more than seven million people dying prematurely due to pollution. About 90 percent of the world population breathes air that contains levels of pollutants that exceed guidelines set by the World Health Organization (WHO). The 2023 "State of the Air" report sponsored by the America Lung Association reveals that nearly 36 percent of Americans (almost 120 million people) live in places with unhealthy levels of air pollution. Furthermore, people of color are disproportionately affected by air pollution, composing 72 percent of the 18 million Americans living in counties with the worst air quality. One United Nations study claims that exposure to air pollution is the largest cause of disease and premature death in the world, taking the lives of 7 million persons each year. In the United States, air pollution causes more deaths each year than murders and car accidents combined.

In his groundbreaking encyclical *Laudato si'*, Pope Francis recognizes the pollution problem in a graphic image: "The earth, our home, is beginning to look more and more like an immense pile of filth" (no. 21). In many places, "beautiful landscapes are now covered with rubbish" and landfills are overflowing. The pope links the pollution problem to a "throwaway culture" that casually disposes of everything not immediately useful. He cites one example: "Most of the paper we produce is thrown away and not recycled" (no. 22). He laments that our industrial system "has not yet managed to adopt a circular model of production capable of preserving resources for present and future generations." To counteract the throwaway culture, we should limit as much as possible "the use of non-renewable resources, moderating their consumption, maximizing their efficient use, reusing and recycling them" (no. 22).

In 2021, Francis launched a seven-year "Laudato Si' Action Platform" with seven specific goals, beginning with a new effort to hear the cries of the earth. In announcing the plan, the pope said that we must resist the temptation to be "predators of resources," adding that "from God's hands we have received a garden, we cannot leave a desert to our children."[1]

By highlighting recycling as a response to the cries of the earth, Francis provides moral support for prominent environmental agencies in the United States urging more Americans to recycle. For example, the Environmental Protection Agency (EPA) reports that only about 32 percent of Americans recycle regularly today. This is up from less than 7 percent in 1960, but still far from what is needed to preserve our common home. The EPA claims that "reused activities" account for 681,000 jobs and $37 billion in wages. The agency highlights the annual celebration of "America Recycles Day" on November 15 as a way of encouraging all Americans to "recycle right" on a regular basis. Recycling has many benefits: reducing the amount of waste sent to landfills and incinerators, conserving natural resources, preventing pollution, saving energy, conserving valuable resources, and providing new jobs. Finally, the EPA encourages all Americans to learn how to recycle properly in their local communities.

With Pope Francis, we ask God to "bring healing to our lives that we may sow beauty, not pollution and destruction" (*Laudato si'* no. 246).

Question: How can I improve my recycling practices?

The Threat of Water Pollution

The United Nations Environment Programme (UNEP), charged with protecting the earth, lists water pollution as one of the major threats to the inhabitants of our common home. Unsafe water kills more people each year than war and all other forms of violence combined. Furthermore, the world is facing a problem of water scarcity, since less than 1 percent of the earth's freshwater is available for human use. Water resources, including streams, rivers, underground estuaries, ground water, and lakes have been polluted by toxic substances from farms, cities, and factories.

Although the United States has the safest drinking water in the world, polluted water still causes over seven million illnesses each year. Fifty years after the 1972 Clean Water Act, administered by the Environmental Protection Agency (EPA), U.S. waterways are still severely polluted, with about half of the area of our rivers, streams, underground estuaries, and lakes across the country no longer safe for swimming, fishing, or drinking. According to an estimate by the Centers for Disease Control (CDC), each year water-based pathogens in the United States cause 7,000 deaths, 120,000 hospitalizations, 7 million illnesses, and 3 billion dollars in health care costs.

Oceans and seas, which cover 70 percent of the earth and provide essential food, energy, and water, are endangered by human activity that continues to contaminate the planet's largest ecosystem, affecting the livelihoods of billions of people. For example, according to a United Nations report, more than 17 million metric tons of plastic entered our oceans in 2021. Plastic pollution that accounts for 85 percent of ocean litter poses a threat to coral reefs, the fishing industry, marine life, and to the health of human beings around the globe who consume seafood contaminated by plastic particles.

In his encyclical *Laudato si'* and subsequent commentaries, Pope Francis addresses the problem of water pollution from a moral and social justice perspective. Morally, he states, "Access to safe drinkable water is a basic and universal right, since it is essential to human survival" (no. 30). The world owes a "grave social debt" to the poor that can be partly paid by increased funding to provide clean water and sanitary services for developing countries with poor levels of water. In water-abundant countries, where water continues to be wasted, the pope suggests we develop educational programs and cultural adaptations that will promote responsible water conservation.

The EPA provides a long list of practical tips for conserving water. In the bathroom, for example, we can take shorter showers, draw less water for baths, and turn off the water while brushing teeth and shaving. In the kitchen and laundry, we can compost food scraps rather than use a garbage disposal, run the washing machine with full loads of clothes.

Outdoors, we can water grass in the evening or very early in the morning to minimize evaporation, and use a broom instead of a hose to clean off the driveway or sidewalk. We can all learn from our sisters and brothers who have found creative ways to conserve water.

With Pope Francis, we thank God for "Sister Water," and pray that "water may not be a sign of separation between peoples, but of encounter for the human community."[2]

Question: What more can I do to conserve water?

Biodiversity Loss

"Biodiversity loss impacts food supplies and access to clean water—without it we have no future on our planet."[3] This dire assessment comes from a report by the United Nations Environment Programme. The report attributes this loss to the human impact on the environment in the past half century causing a "catastrophic decline" in the earth's biodiversity unprecedented in human history. Over the past fifty years, the earth has lost two-thirds of its wildlife and over 80 percent of its freshwater population. Modern science tells us that there are some 8 million animal and plant species on earth, with about 1 million threatened with extinction, many within decades.

Healthy biodiverse ecosystems contribute to the well-being of our common home and its citizens. For example, intact wetlands help filter out contaminants, so that they do not enter our waterways. Soil rich in organic matter helps prevent flood damage and boosts agricultural yield. Preserved rainforests—the home of many indigenous species—keep open the possibility of developing nature-based medicines that benefit the whole human family.

Deforestation, accelerated by human activity (especially agriculture), is the major source of biodiversity loss and the impairment of ecosystems. For example, corporations make a profit turning large sections of the Amazon rainforest into cattle ranches to satisfy the worldwide desire for beef. Likewise, commercial overfishing is a major threat to marine life, putting many species at risk of extinction.

In his 128-page encyclical, *Laudato si'*, Pope Francis devotes almost five pages to the loss of biodiversity. He begins by blaming "short-sighted" commercial enterprises which "plunder" the earth's resources. The depletion of forests and wetlands entails the loss of species that have "infinite value as God's creatures." Because of human activity, "thousands of species will no longer give glory to God by their very existence, nor convey their message to us" (no. 33).

Francis warns against excessive, destructive human interventions in nature. "We seem to think that we can substitute an irreplaceable and irretrievable beauty with something we have created ourselves." The pope castigates developers who exploit nature for economic benefits and perpetrate "terrible injustices" against vulnerable peoples and poor persons. We must not be "silent witnesses" to injustices that make "the rest of humanity, present and future, pay the extremely high costs of environmental deterioration" (no. 36).

Pope Francis lauds countries that have established sanctuaries on land and in the oceans that prohibit human intervention. He urges the world to pay special attention to protecting areas vital to the health of the earth, such as rainforests and coral reefs, each home to huge numbers of unclassified species. Francis reenforces his plea for conserving biodiversity with a reminder that "all creatures are connected" and "all of us as living creatures are dependent on one another" (no. 42).

Various U.S. environmental groups offer suggestions on what ordinary Americans can do to preserve biodiversity: buy produce from local farmers; consume less meat and more plant-based foods; plant local fruits and vegetables in a backyard or hanging garden; buy more organically produced food, even though it may be more expensive and harder to identify; and respect parks and nature preserves.

Pope Francis invites us to pray in the "great cathedral of creation" and "revel in the 'grandiose cosmic choir' made up of countless creatures, all singing the praises of God."[4]

Question: What can I do to preserve biodiversity?

Science and Global Warming

A 2022 United Nations report stated that climate change, which involves long-term shifts in temperatures and weather patterns, is "the most pressing issue facing humanity today." Human activities, especially burning the fossil fuels—coal, oil, and natural gas—are contributing to the current severity of droughts, wildfires, and tropical storms. If unchecked, global warming will "completely alter the ecosystems that support life on the planet."[5] Today, there is a near unanimous consensus among scientific experts that global warming is primarily anthropogenic, that is, caused by human activity.

Scientists also help us understand the process of global warming that has increased significantly over the last 1,500 years, and since the beginning of the Industrial Revolution. Burning fossil fuels releases gases, especially carbon dioxide, and creates a "greenhouse effect," forming a shield that keeps the heat reflected off the earth from dispersing into space. The heat trapped in the atmosphere causes temperatures on earth to rise (global warming) that leads to climate change.

In 1988, the United Nations established the International Panel on Climate Change (IPCC) charged with examining the relevant scientific literature and producing Assessment Reports to guide official policy decisions. This process led the UN to set the goal of limiting global warming to 1.5 degrees Celsius (2.7 degrees Fahrenheit) above preindustrial levels—a goal generally accepted by most nations in the 2015 Paris Agreement.

On March 20, 2023, the IPCC issued a nearly eight-thousand-page comprehensive summary of the research of hundreds of scientists over the last five years on global warming and climate changes. Here are some of its main findings.

- There is a scientific consensus that human-caused global warming, which has already reached 1.1 degree Celsius above preindustrial levels, is causing climate extremes such as flooding and wildfires that disproportionally harm developing regions and poor people all over the world.
- The continuing emission of greenhouse gases at the current rate will push us to the 1.5-degree Celsius ceiling sometime between 2030 and 2035.
- The report estimates how much worse the situation will be if warming passes the 1.5-degree Celsius ceiling and rises to 2 degrees Celsius. Three times as many people would be exposed regularly to extreme heat, the rise of

sea levels would be 0.06 meters higher by 2100, twice as many plant and animal species would be lost, and marine fisheries would see catches decline twice as much as crop yields, leading to food insecurity in some areas.

- Finally, the UN report states that we have the knowledge and resources to limit global warming and avoid the worst of the climate catastrophes. However, the window of opportunity is limited, perhaps a decade, and all nations must act swiftly and decisively to avert catastrophic harm to the earth and its inhabitants.

In *Laudato si'*, Pope Francis recognizes a "very solid scientific consensus" that most global warming in recent decades is due to the "great concentration of greenhouse gases," "released mainly as a result of human activities" (no. 23). He stresses the urgency of the crisis: "Doomsday predictions can no longer be met with irony or disdain" but must propel us into constructive action to save our planet.

According to a 2022 Pew Research poll, only 54 percent of adult Catholics in the United States agree with the pope's position on anthropogenic global warming, with 25 percent saying that it is due to natural patterns and 9 percent denying that the earth is warming. Four out of ten Catholics who attend Mass regularly say their homilist never mentions climate change. Clearly, Pope Francis has not yet been able to convince large numbers of U.S. Catholics—clergy and laity—to join him in accepting the scientific consensus. Mindful that more must be done, in 2021, the pope launched a new seven-year *Laudato si'* action plan, designed to overcome selfishness and indifference and to promote a lifestyle and a society that is "finally eco-sustainable."

Inspired by Pope Francis, let us thank God for scientists and their amazing accomplishments that help us better understand, appreciate, respect, and care for our earth that speaks of God's love and is, in its diversity, a "caress of God."

Question: Do I accept the scientific consensus on global warming, and if so, how would I discuss it with a friend or relative who holds an opposing view?

Global Warming and Christian Hope

The Christian virtue of hope, a gift of the Holy Spirit, empowers us to sustain a balanced, positive effort to limit global warming and save ourselves and our common home. The virtue of hope is different from optimism, whether utopian or reasonable. It is grounded in the faith conviction that God cares for the earth and all its citizens with an unconditional love. Hope avoids the extremes of a paralyzing pessimism ("It's too overwhelming, so I'm not going to think about it") as well as an intentional passivity ("I don't have to do anything because I'm counting on God to intervene and save us"). Concretely, hope moves us to celebrate genuine progress in limiting global warming and to commit ourselves in our own limited way to support further efforts needed to save our common home.

On the positive side, the 2015 Paris Agreement was a major achievement. Most of the countries of the world pledged to reduce voluntarily their emission of greenhouse gases to levels designed to keep global warming below 1.5 degrees Celsius (2.7 degrees Fahrenheit) and to reach carbon-neutral status by the second half of the century. Since each country sets its own target and monitors its progress, there is no way to verify their claims with certainty. However, it remains true that almost all countries recognize that global warming is a major threat to the earth and are willing to take measures to save our planet.

Since 2015, dozens of countries, including the United States and China (the major polluters), have voluntarily submitted stricter pledges. For example, the United States is now committed to cut carbon emissions by about half of the 2005 levels by 2030. The European Union and China have set similar goals to be achieved by 2030. Under President Lula, Brazil, which controls large portions of the Amazon rainforest, recently pledged to reduce deforestation to zero by 2030—a sharp reversal of previous policies. Some U.S. states have set more ambitious goals. For example, California, the fifth-largest economy in the world, has a 2030 goal of cutting emissions by 48 percent compared to its level in 1990.

Many U.S. industries are committed to slowing down global warming. For example, General Motors has joined over 1,000 international companies dedicated to establishing "a safer, greener and better world."[6] GM plans to be carbon neutral by 2040 in its global products and operations.

Most U.S. colleges and universities are committed to reducing their carbon output, and a handful have already achieved "net zero" carbon emissions, also known as "carbon neutrality." For instance, the University of San Francisco, a Jesuit school, reached carbon neutrality in 2019 after a multifaceted approach inspired by Pope Francis, who wrote in *Laudato si'* that "human life is grounded in three fundamental and closely inter-twined relationships: with God, with our neighbour and with the earth itself" (no. 66). The university makes use of solar water heating and does not burn any fossil fuels. To limit the use of cars, the university does not allow student parking on campus, but gives every student a public trans-portation pass. They also offer financial incentives to faculty and staff to use public transportation.

Starting in 1995, the United Nations has sponsored an annual Conference of the Parties (COP) to deal with climate change. These conferences helped prepare for the Paris Agreement and have moni-tored progress ever since. At the 2022 COP 27 conference, the developed nations made tentative pledges to provide financial assistance to help developing countries meet their carbon emission goals.

Christian hope prompts us to celebrate all of these accomplish-ments and more. At the same time, the virtue of hope strengthens us to respond to the new harsh scientific consensus that more must be done to avoid the 1.5-degree Celsius ceiling. Only swift and concerted actions by the nations of the world can save the earth from cataclysmic climate changes. As Americans, we can vote for federal leaders who are not only people of character and competence but who also recognize the problem and support a national effort to save our common home.

Pope Francis encourages us to express our Christian hope by fol-lowing the traditional wisdom: "Pray like everything depends on God and act like everything depends on us."[7]

Question: What progress on global warming is most impressive to me?

Global Warming and Ecological Conversion

In response to the major threats to our common home—pollution, biodiversity loss, and especially global warming—Pope Francis has summoned us to an "ecological conversion" leading to the practice of an "integral ecology" needed to save the earth. In *Laudato si'*, Francis begins his treatment of an ecological conversion by noting that some "committed and prayerful Christians" tend to ridicule this concern, while others refuse to change their habits to help fix the problem. As Christians, our relationship with Jesus Christ should guide our relationship to the natural world. Protecting "God's handiwork is essential to a life of virtue not an optional or secondary aspect of our Christian experience" (no. 217). An authentic ecological conversion involves admitting ways we have harmed God's creation by our actions and by our omissions. It recognizes the power of a "utilitarian mindset" and an "unethical consumerism" to blunt our "ecological awareness." And it is rooted in a growing appreciation of the intrinsic value of God's creation and our responsibility to care for it.

Francis places his call for an ecological conversion in the context of the long and rich tradition of Christian spirituality consistently committed to living gospel-inspired faith convictions in the real world. The pope insists that a "passionate concern for the protection of our world" cannot be "sustained by doctrine alone" but requires a "change of heart" that "encourages, motivates, nourishes and gives meaning" (no. 216) to all our efforts to protect the earth and all its citizens.

For Pope Francis, ecological conversion informed by Christian faith is not an end in itself but an important catalyst for achieving an "integral ecology" that includes an ideal moral vision to guide a worldwide effort to promote the common good of the earth and all its citizens. Applying his fundamental conviction that "everything is closely united," Francis insists that "we are faced not with two separate crises, one environmental and the other social, but rather with one complex crisis which is both social and environmental." He grounds his analysis in reality: "We are part of nature, included in it and therefore, in constant interaction with it." Thus, we need "comprehensive solutions which consider the interactions within natural systems themselves and with social systems." Concretely this means "combating poverty, restoring dignity to the excluded, and at the same time protecting nature" (no. 139).

Pope Francis sees an integral ecology in its diverse elements serving the common good in various ways: strengthening societal institutions, especially the family; protecting indigenous communities from exploitation of their homelands and their distinctive cultures; keeping God's gift of creation intact for the next generation; practicing the preferential option for the poor, who suffer the most from ecological degradation; working for a more equal distribution of the world's goods that promotes peace, stability, and security for all people; protecting the cultural treasures of humanity; and developing living spaces (homes, worksites, common areas, and cities) that help humanize daily life. In sum, Pope Francis has called all Christians to an ecological conversion so that we can be leaven for the world as a whole, striving for the integral ecology needed to save us and our common home.

With Pope Francis, we pray: "All-powerful God....You embrace with your tenderness all that exists. Pour out upon us the power of your love, that we may protect life and beauty.... Encourage us, we pray, in our struggle for justice, love and peace" (no. 246).

Question: What concrete step can I take to facilitate my ecological conversion?

7

HUMANIZING WORK

The Role of Labor Unions

Sue, a married woman in her late fifties with adult children, is a longtime employee of the John Deere company and a member of the United Auto Workers union. After long and unsuccessful negotiations, she voted with 99 percent of her 10,000-member union to go on strike on October 14, 2021, for higher pay and better benefits. She wanted to be in solidarity with younger employees seeking to preserve a pension option, and she believed a substantial pay increase was overdue, especially since John Deere anticipated a record annual profit of over $5.7 billion. During the strike, Sue took her turn walking the picket line in increasingly cold weather, while trying to get by on the union's $275 weekly strike pay and limited medical insurance. She was grateful for the assistance provided by UAW locals around the country and by local businesses, who provided free food and goods. When union and company negotiators reached an agreement on November 18, 2021, providing a 10 percent pay raise and other benefits, Sue felt the sacrifices she made were well worth it.

Labor unions in the United States have a long history of improving the wages and benefits of American workers. The American Federation of Labor (AFL), founded in 1886 and led by Samuel Gompers until his death in 1924, played a major role in coordinating strikes to benefit workers. The Wagner Act, signed into law in 1935, established the legal right of most workers to organize and join unions to bargain collectively and initiate strikes. That same year, the two largest unions—the AFL and the Congress of Industrial Organizations (CIO)—merged, representing about 35 percent of American workers. Since then, unions have lost membership and now represent only about 11 percent of the labor force.

MEDITATIONS ON CATHOLIC SOCIAL TEACHING

Ever since Pope Leo XIII's groundbreaking 1891 encyclical, *Rerum novarum*, Catholic Social Teaching has consistently supported labor unions. For example, in Pope John Paul II's important encyclical *Laborem exercens*, he insists that labor unions are an "indispensable element" of modern societies and the struggle for social justice (no. 20). In their 1986 pastoral letter, *Economic Justice for All*, the American bishops taught that our changing economy "requires a strong role for labor unions," to ensure the rights of workers through "collective negotiation" (no. 303).

The Compendium of the Social Doctrine of the Church, first published by the Vatican in 2005, recognizes the important role of unions in defending the vital interests of workers and promoting the struggle for social justice and in working for the proper arrangement of economic life (nos. 306–7). In pursuit of these goals, labor unions have the historically hard-earned right to strike, a "collective and concentrated refusal on the part of workers to continue to render their services" (no. 304). Strikes are legitimate under certain conditions: when they seek a "proportionate benefit," for example, better working conditions and a more just wage; when they are the last resort after all other methods have been ineffective; and when they are conducted by peaceful methods and violence is avoided.

The American bishops, who have historically provided strong support for the labor movement, have also insisted that unions have proper duties and responsibilities. For example, their pastoral letter, *Economic Justice for All*, insists that union leaders have the responsibility to preserve the good name of the union movement. Unions should present demands that serve the common good and do not harm the rights of more vulnerable members of society. They should exercise leadership in the struggle against racial and sexual discrimination that has blotted the record of some unions and provide education and training to keep workers employable (cf. no. 106). In general, Catholic Social Teaching has consistently supported the labor movement while offering moral guidance on how unions can contribute to the common good.

Question: What part of Sue's story is most impressive to me and how does it exemplify Catholic Social Teaching?

Balancing Work and Leisure

Don is a forty-year-old happily married man with two young children. After earning a college degree in international relations, he dedicated himself to his work recruiting international students to enroll in American universities. His business grew rapidly, enabling him to hire over one hundred employees. He traveled four months a year, visited forty-five countries and had contacts in major cities around the world. With his wife and growing family, he lived abroad for a few years and then moved to Boston, from which he continued his extensive travels.

In December 2019, Don and his wife, who also could do her demanding job from home, decided to move back to Toledo, Ohio, where they could raise their two boys in familiar surroundings close to their extended families, while he continued his international travels. Just months later, the COVID-19 pandemic decimated much of Don's international business, forcing him to disband his whole team. Grateful that he himself still has work, he recruits international students virtually, from his home.

Don has made the most of his changed situation. It is clearer to him now that family has a proper priority over business. He now typically fixes breakfast for his sons, takes an afternoon walk with his wife, and generally tries to be attentive to family needs. He also takes better care of his own health, exercising regularly, doing some gardening, and relieving stress by turning off his phone for hours at a time. With less time spent on his recruiting job, Don is free to do volunteer work in his local community that he finds very fulfilling.

Many Americans struggle to achieve a healthy relationship between work and leisure. According to one market research study, 48 percent of employed Americans think of themselves as "workaholics," and 53 percent report being stressed over work. Some actually are addicted to work—about 10 percent of workers according to one psychological study. Over 10 percent of Americans work more than fifty hours per week—the poor, because they are working multiple jobs, and the well-paid, because they choose to put in extra hours. A 2019 Rand Corporation study found that average Americans have over five hours of free time each day, but most of that time is spent watching screens and only 7 percent doing healthy physical activities.

Catholic Social Teaching warns us against some dangerous temptations: identifying ourselves with our work, making an idol out of work, giving work priority over family, and becoming addicted to work. We are God's handiwork, called to share in God's ongoing creative activity. Work should help us develop our talents and gifts and become whole integrated persons. A healthy life should include both work and leisure that nourishes the soul and provides bodily rest.

The *Compendium of Social Doctrines of the Church* grounds these admonitions on the scriptural command and practice of the "Sabbath rest," which it calls the "epitome of biblical teaching on work." The Lord's Day provides an opportunity to thank God for blessings and to attend to family concerns. It also serves as a "barrier against becoming slaves to work" (no. 258). For Christians, work enables us to share in the mission of Christ, the carpenter turned preacher, to humanize the world. Work provides us with daily opportunities to grow in holiness. We can transform the toilsome, fatiguing, and burdensome aspects of work by uniting with Christ, who embraced the cross, leading to a fuller, glorified life.

Question: How does Don's story exemplify Catholic Social Teaching on work and leisure?

A Just Wage for Underpaid Workers

Bill is a sixty-eight-year-old man who worked hard for many years as a self-employed roofer and raised his three children by living frugally and carefully managing his limited income. In his early sixties, health problems forced him to give up his roofing business. Desperate for employment, he took a job with a company in Cleveland delivering caskets to major cities around the state of Ohio. On a typical day, he gets up at 3:00 a.m., drives thirty-five minutes to the factory, loads caskets on a truck, spends about seven hours delivering them to funeral homes around the state, and arrives back home in the afternoon. For this, he is paid $12 an hour with no benefits or health insurance. It costs him almost one hundred dollars a month in gas and tolls just to get to work and back home. He does get two weeks paid vacation and uses his long hours in the truck to listen to Christian radio stations. During the pandemic, he continued to work but had to take unpaid time off to care for his wife, a retired schoolteacher, who became seriously ill. Getting ever further behind financially and angry with the way his boss treats him, he looked at many other job openings caused by the pandemic, but at his age he could not find anything better. Bill is trapped in a challenging situation with a job he cannot quit that still leaves him and his wife living below the government poverty line.

According to government statistics about 2.7 percent of Americans are classified as "working poor," usually employed full time. Among part-time workers, 9.8 percent are living below the poverty line. They are part of what is called the "precariat," a social class of underpaid workers who live constantly in precarious circumstances.

The *Compendium* states that a "just wage is the legitimate fruit of work" and that "remuneration is the most important means for achieving justice in work relationships." A just wage enables a worker to "cultivate worthily his own material, social, cultural and spiritual life and that of his dependents" (no. 302). The simple agreement between employee and employer on pay is not sufficient to qualify as a just wage, which "must not be below the level of subsistence" needed by workers. "Natural justice precedes and is above the freedom of the contract" (no. 302).

For over a century, the American bishops have argued that full-time workers have a right to a "just wage" that allows them to provide a "dignified livelihood" for their family. They have also supported universal health care, unemployment compensation, and paid sick leave designed to enable workers and their families to lead a full and dignified life.

Question: Does the Catholic teaching on the ideal of a just wage influence my outlook on practical policies such as the proper amount of a mandated minimum wage?

Celebrating Homemakers and Family Life

Jill is a committed Catholic, happily married woman in her sixties, a mother of four with seven grandchildren. She has devoted her life to the crucial work of homemaking, raising children, and caring for her family. After earning a degree in education, she took a job teaching English in a local high school that brought her great satisfaction and enough income to support herself. Three years into her teaching career, she fell in love, got married a year later, and formed a mutually enriching partnership that has lasted almost forty years.

When Jill became pregnant, she and her husband made a mutual decision that she would quit the teaching job she loved and work full time attending to the home and children, while he maintained his lucrative job to support the family—an agreement that has worked well for both of them. Jill has never regretted her decision or felt that something was missing in her life. On the contrary, she has found fulfillment in being a loving mother and grandmother. She has enjoyed the challenge of meeting each child's distinctive needs, making holidays and birthdays memorable, and maintaining peace and harmony in the family. With the cooperation of her husband, she has done her best to pass on her Catholic faith to her children, mostly by example, sometimes by words. She made sure they attended Sunday Mass regularly, prayed before meals, did Lenten penances, and participated in family efforts to help the poor. She is disappointed that her oldest son no longer goes to Mass, but finds a measure of comfort knowing that he has solid values and is in the hands of a merciful God. For her adult children, she remains a caring mother, ready to listen and help when needed. She thanks God for her grandchildren, who gladden her heart and keep her young in spirit.

Unfortunately, homemaking does not always enjoy the respect it deserves. A materialistic culture that values having things has difficulty appreciating the sacrifice homemakers make in raising their children and the skills needed to meet their individual needs. The tendency to equate work with a paying job leads to the common statement that homemakers do not work. Actually, if they were paid $14 per hour for the various services they provide, they would make more than $130,000 per year, according to one estimate.

Catholic Social Teaching describes work as legitimate, purposeful, planned activities that promote the common good and personal growth: that includes homemaking and raising children! It also emphasizes the importance of healthy families in promoting personal development and the good of society. Families are "the first natural society," the building blocks of society, and they serve as a "domestic church" according to Vatican II's Dogmatic Constitution on the Church, *Lumen gentium* (no. 11). In the give and take of family life, we learn that genuine love is patient and kind, ready to forgive and seek reconciliation. A stable family allows children to develop fundamental trust and the ability to sacrifice for the good of others. In this regard, Pope Francis calls mothers "a great treasure," because they are an "antidote to individualism," which is toxic for community life, including families.

Question: Do I respect and appreciate the crucial work of homemakers and how could I express my gratitude?

Volunteer Service

Anita, a financially comfortable widow in her eighties, has done volunteer work for almost two decades at Helping Hands, a social ministry on the east side of Toledo, Ohio, originally established in 1982 by St. Louis Catholic Parish under the leadership of Fr. Robert Armstrong. It now provides a soup kitchen, food pantry, and clothing center for persons in the area in need of assistance. After recovering from a difficult time in her own life, Anita was moved to help less fortunate persons served by Helping Hands. Encouraged by their open, respectful, nonjudgmental staff, Anita began by organizing piles of donated shoes so that those in need could more easily find a suitable pair. Next, she took on the task of organizing the many piles of clothing donated to the center. By 2011, she succeeded in establishing a clothing center in the now-unused church building, where donated clothing was marked and hung on racks for easy, dignified shopping for the more than 500 individuals who come each month. Even with the diminishments of age and the challenges of the pandemic, Anita, who is very modest about her achievements, kept working at Helping Hands a couple days a week for about five hours per day, continuing to add to the over ten thousand volunteer hours she has already logged.

About 25 percent of Americans spend at least fifty hours a year doing volunteer work, enabling many faith-based nonprofits to maintain their extensive charitable work. Some studies indicate that the pandemic produced an increase in volunteer work, as good people came together to help people suffering from the common health threat.

The *Compendium of the Social Doctrine of the Church* makes the crucial distinction between an "objective sense of work," that concentrates on what is done or accomplished and a "subjective sense," that emphasizes how work impacts workers themselves (cf. nos. 270–73). As humans made in the image of God, we are capable of directing our lives and actualizing our potential. The worth of work is based primarily not on the type of work done but on the essential dignity of the persons doing the work. Since the human person is the "measure of the dignity of work," all work has an "ethical voice of its own," even if it is considered "the merest service" (no. 273). Furthermore, work has an "intrinsic social dimension" since it involves "doing something for someone else," which offers occasions for "exchanges, relationships and encounters" (no. 273).

On several occasions, Pope Francis has praised volunteers, calling them "precious resources of the Church" who "silently and unassumingly give shape and visibility to mercy."[1] He has also called volunteers the "strength of the Church" who function as a "shocking force" that challenges the selfish ways of the world. They are a "dimension of the Church's mission," giving concrete expression to Christ's command to care for his brothers and sisters in need. The pope views volunteering as a "grace from God" and urges volunteers to carry on their important work with courage and perseverance. Finally, Pope Francis reminds us to express gratitude for the generous service of volunteer workers.[2]

Question: How do I feel about volunteering my time and energy to serve others?

8

OVERCOMING RACISM

What Is Racism?

In 2018, the American bishops published a pastoral letter, *Open Wide Our Hearts: The Enduring Call to Love*, which remains a valuable religious and moral guide to overcoming the racism that continues to affect our country. The pastoral letter recognizes racism as United States' "original sin" and describes it as a "conviction or attitude" that one's own race is superior to other races that are deemed inferior and unworthy of equal regard. This distorted attitude can lead to sinful actions that exclude, ridicule, mistreat, or unjustly discriminate against persons based on their race. Racist acts are objectively sinful because they violate the natural law by not giving others their just due and by failing to acknowledge the inherent dignity of other persons. From a Christian perspective, they are sinful because they violate Christ's command to love our neighbor. Fear and hatred of others can arise when we forget the fundamental scriptural truth that all people are our brothers and sisters, sharing a common origin "equally made in the image of God."

The pastoral letter recalls the biblical story of Cain, who forgot this truth and killed his brother Abel (Gen 4:1–16). It also quotes the Apostle John: "All who hate a brother or sister are murderers, and you know that murderers do not have eternal life abiding in them" (1 John 3:15). Racism also includes sins of omission, when individuals and churches remain silent and fail to act when encountering racial injustice. The bishops acknowledge that the sin of racism, which denies the fundamental dignity of all God's people, "persists in our lives, in our country, and in our world." It is manifested in unjust housing restrictions, limited educational opportunities, and high incarceration rates of Black citizens.

The pastoral letter recognizes that we still suffer from "institutional racism," which arises from practices and traditions that treat certain groups unjustly. It explains that "the cumulative effects of personal sins of racism have led to social structures of injustice and violence." Upbringing and culture can infect our hearts with racist attitudes without our conscious knowledge or consent. Unconscious prejudice can lead to racist actions that we do not recognize as evil but which demean others and deny their just rights and benefits as citizens. As a prime example of systemic racism, the pastoral mentions the Flint water crisis, which exposed thousands of children in Flint, Michigan, to lead poisoning beginning in 2014, when the city switched its drinking water supply from the Detroit system to the Flint River in a cost-saving move. This disaster resulted from policy decisions that denied needed resources to update the water system in a segregated, majority African American community.

Finally, the American bishops who have consistently opposed abortion, euthanasia, and assisted suicide as intrinsic evils unequivocally declared that "racism is a life issue," indicating that it is also an intrinsic evil that violates human dignity. This important declaration highlights both the grave moral evil of racism and our personal responsibility to do what we can to overcome it.

Question: What element of the bishops' teaching is most helpful to me in understanding racism?

Education

The American bishops' pastoral letter *Open Wide Our Hearts* lists discrimination in educational opportunities as one of the ongoing unjust manifestations of systemic racism in the United States. Historically, slave owners in the Southern states made every effort to keep their slaves illiterate, even imposing stiff penalties on any white persons teaching slaves to read. By the time the Thirteenth Amendment officially abolished slavery in 1865, only 4 percent of enslaved persons could read or write.

After reconstruction ended in 1877, the Confederate states passed restrictive "Black Codes" that legalized segregation and denied African American citizens the right to attend public schools. In the infamous 1896 *Plessy v. Ferguson* decision, the Supreme Court declared that the protections of the Fourteenth Amendment apply to political and civil rights but not to "social rights" like sitting in the railroad car of one's choice or attending the school of one's choice. This ruling effectively enshrined the "separate but equal" justification for segregating public schools.

African Americans in the South did their best to create their own school systems, severely hampered by a lack of funds and a limited pool of trained teachers. In this regard, the bishops' pastoral letter raised up the outstanding example of Sister Katherine Drexel (1858–1955), the first saint born a U.S. citizen, who founded fifty schools for African American students, including Xavier University of Louisiana, the first and only Catholic university in the United States specifically for Black citizens. It was Drexel's admonition to "open wide our hearts" in serving others that provided the title for the bishops' pastoral letter.

In the 1954 *Brown v. Board of Education* case, the Supreme Court overturned the Plessy decision by declaring that segregating students in public schools based on race was unconstitutional. The subsequent attempts to desegregate public schools through busing were extremely controversial and in most cases ineffective. The Civil Rights Act of 1964 did help the process by making it easier to file lawsuits against discriminatory practices and by providing funds for local school boards to assist their desegregation efforts.

Various studies show that Black students have made progress educationally but still lag behind white students. For example, a Pew Research Study reported that, in 1993, 14 percent more white teenagers had a high school diploma than Black teenagers, and by 2017 that gap was cut in half with 94 percent of white students graduating from high school as opposed to 87 percent of Black students. During that same span, the Black college graduation rate doubled from 12 percent to 24 percent, but still lagged behind the rate for white students, which went from 24 percent to 33 percent during that time.

The bishops' pastoral letter reminds us that Christ's command to love our neighbor impels us to work for justice. There are various ways of applying this moral imperative to helping racial minority students in disadvantaged schools. For example, a person could tutor a student in reading who does not receive that education at home; donate school supplies to needy students in inner city grade schools; participate in a program to help struggling students finish high school; mentor a student who wants to be the first in the family to attend college; and support local efforts to establish prekindergarten programs that are absolutely crucial for the long-term academic success of racial minority students.

Question: In what ways can I personally "open wide my heart" to my Black brothers and sisters seeking educational justice?

Voting Rights and Political Power

After the Civil War (1861–65), Black activists worked diligently to secure voting rights for freed Black slaves. During the decade known as Radical Reconstruction (1867–77), Congress passed legislation granting Black Americans the rights of citizenship (the Thirteenth Amendment ratified in 1865), due process under the law (the Fourteenth Amendment ratified in 1870), and the right to vote (the Fifteenth Amendment ratified in 1870). Despite this progress, Southern states found ways to restrict Black voting by enforcing laws requiring literacy tests and poll taxes. The Ku Klux Klan, which was established in 1865, was a loosely organized group of political and social terrorists whose goals included the maintenance and promotion of absolute white supremacy in response to newly gained civil and political rights by southern Blacks after the Civil War. They relied on violent tactics, including lynchings, to intimidate Black citizens and prevent them from voting.

These devious tactics were very successful in suppressing Black voting in the Southern states and limiting the number of Black office holders. For example, in 1965, there were no Black senators and only six Blacks in the U.S. House. Only 2 percent of the 15,000 eligible Black voters in Selma, Alabama, voted that year.

On Sunday, March 7, 1965, Martin Luther King led a group of six hundred activists on a march from Selma heading for Montgomery, the state capital, to register to vote. Shortly after departing Selma, state troopers viciously attacked the peaceful marchers, forcing them to return to Selma. The brutal attack, recorded on television, caught the attention of President Lyndon Johnson, members of Congress and religious leaders around the country. Fueled by public outrage, Congress passed the 1967 Voting Rights Act that outlawed literacy tests and effectively ended poll taxes, making registration and voting easier for Black citizens. Results were dramatic. In Mississippi, for example, the percentage of Black citizens who voted increased from 6 percent in 1964 to almost 60 percent in 1969.

As the American bishops said in *Open Wide Our Hearts*, we have made significant progress on overcoming racism in our country, but there is much more to be done. For instance, in 2023, we have fifty-nine Black representatives in the House but only three senators. There are numerous Black mayors, including those who have served in our largest cities, New York, Los Angeles, Chicago, and Houston, but only three African Americans have been elected governor. Most striking on the positive side is that we twice elected a Black man, Barack Obama, as president. Perhaps influenced by the presence of a Black woman, Kamala Harris, on the ballot in 2020, almost 50 percent of eligible Black voters actually voted that year, matching the percentages of white voters who cast a ballot. We have indeed made progress but, as the bishops remind us, that should spur us to strive even harder to overcome the evils of racism, our nation's original sin.

When Pope Francis addressed the U.S. Congress in 2015, he raised up Dr. Martin Luther King Jr., who led the Selma march fifty years ago, as an inspiration for all of us. He praised King for inspiring us with his dream of "full civil and political rights,"—"dreams which lead to action, to participation, to commitment," which "awaken what is deepest and truest in the life of a people."[1] Amen.

Question: Does reflecting on these mixed developments energize or depress me?

Affirmative Action

On June 29, 2023, the Supreme Court struck down affirmative action programs at Harvard and the University of North Carolina. The Court effectively overturned a previous ruling that universities could consider race in their admissions process in order to combat historic discrimination against minorities. Harvard's argument in the case highlighted the value of a diverse student body in which everyone benefits from a range of perspectives in the classroom. Under its affirmative action policy, Harvard, which admits only 4 percent of applicants, had by 2021 achieved a diverse undergraduate student body that was over 14 percent African American. In an amicus brief filed in the Harvard case, University of California chancellors said that when California banned affirmative action policies in 1996, there was a huge drop in diversity at its state's elite universities and that alternative approaches have fallen short of achieving racially diverse campus environments.

The Supreme Court decision generated a variety of responses. In dissent in the North Carolina case, Justice Jackson called the majority decision unjust, a tragedy for us all that will hamper our elite universities from a diverse student population to the benefit of every American. Harvard vowed to look for other ways to achieve a racially diverse student population. Leaders of Historically Black Colleges and Universities (HBCUs) suggested that their schools will now draw a greater number of talented Black students, prompting the Brookings Institute to call for greater investment in HBCUs by corporations, philanthropies, and individuals.

The American bishops responded to the Supreme Court decision by reaffirming their support for affirmative action. In their 1979 pastoral letter, *Brothers and Sisters to Us*, the bishops recognized that an "unresolved racism permeates our society's structures and resides in the hearts of many among the majority." In this context, the bishops endorsed "affirmative action as a constructive way of addressing" the long-standing imbalance in minority representation on our campuses. In their 1986 pastoral letter, *Economic Justice for All*, the bishops again endorsed affirmative action policies. They argued that all persons have a right to participate in society and where the effects of past discrimination persist, society has the obligation to overcome the "legacy of injustice." In meeting this obligation, "judiciously administered affirmative action programs in education" play an important role in achieving the participation that is "at the heart of true justice."

Through their Ad Hoc Committee against Racism, the bishops noted that education is a "gift and an opportunity" not always within the reach of marginalized racial minorities. They promised that Catholic universities would continue their efforts to make education possible and affordable for everyone.

The Association of Catholic Colleges and Universities (ACCU) blasted the decision for undermining the decade-long work of higher education to find solutions to the social evil of racism. The ACCU went on to declare that it would "continue to be guided by Catholic social teaching" to increase minority representation on our campuses. Seattle University, a Jesuit school, suggested that the Court's ruling raised questions about how the university can remain faithful to its Jesuit, Catholic values in recruiting and retaining a diverse student body.

Catholic Social Teaching supports affirmative action for several reasons: racism is a continuing problem that calls Christians to search for effective solutions; the victims of racism are underrepresented on college campuses; a diverse student body benefits all students; and a work force that includes highly educated, talented minorities serves the good of the whole society.

Question: What do I think of the arguments for affirmative action?

White Privilege

In her book *White Fragility*, sociologist Robin DiAngelo encourages white liberals, people like herself, to overcome their instinctive reluctance to face the systemic racism that automatically grants them "white privilege." She claims that white progressives who do not recognize their privileged position cause deadly damage to people of color by perpetuating the "color blindness" argument that race does not matter, and which prevents society from seeing how much it does.

In 2013, the respected moral theologian Charles Curran wrote an autobiographical essay confessing that through much of his theological career he was "blatantly unaware of his own white privilege." He prided himself on going out of his way to support African American students working on their doctorates and Black theologians giving presentations at conferences, quite satisfied that he was doing what he could to counter systemic racism. He credited a Black female theologian, M. Shawn Copeland, with raising his consciousness on racism. Fundamentally, he thought of himself as the subject who was graciously doing what he could to help "them," an approach that "absolutized" his own limited position, making others the "object of my good will." He saw his own white theological standpoint as normative for judging all other perspectives.

Drawing on Copeland's appropriation of the astute analysis of various conversions by Canadian Jesuit Bernard Lonergan, Curran began a process of "personal conversion" that recognized the privilege he enjoyed throughout his life. For example, he had parents who encouraged him to study and sent him to excellent Catholic schools taught by dedicated sisters, and the Church paid for all his college theology and doctoral studies, relieving him of the need to have a job and carrying the burden of student loans—a privilege enjoyed by very few others.

In addition to a personal conversion, Curran began a process of "intellectual conversion" that enabled him to see the limitations of his own culturally conditioned theological perspective as well as what he could learn from the distinctive perspectives of African American theologians.

Finally, Curran spoke of a "spiritual conversion" that, for him, meant recalling a forgotten truth that American society is threatened by social sins, including racism. This enabled him to see how racial bias is embedded in societal institutions, which produce false consciousness oblivious to the plight of victims. Charles Curran concluded by saying that he hopes to learn more about racism from dialogue with Black theologians and their distinctive experiences of systemic racism.

Although the American bishops have not directly addressed the problem of white privilege, they have provided in their pastoral letter, *Open Wide Our Hearts*, some helpful points to guide further reflection. They note that, for many people, the real problem is not overt racism but the temptation to assume an attitude of superiority toward others. They remind us of the fundamental biblical truth that all people possess an intrinsic worth and dignity because they are made in the image and likeness of God. And they encourage us to reflect on the life and example of Jesus Christ, who taught us to love our neighbor as ourself.

Question: What is my reaction to the claim that white Americans enjoy "white privilege?"

9

CAPITAL PUNISHMENT

The Case For

In 2002 the highly respected Jesuit theologian, Avery Dulles, published an article, "Catholics and Capital Punishment," in *First Things* that still serves as an excellent summary of the arguments for the right of states to execute criminals. Avery Dulles, who was installed as a cardinal in 2001 and died in 2008 at the age of ninety, noted that the Mosaic law identified thirty-six capital offenses, including idolatry and murder, that merited execution. In the New Testament, the right of the state to put criminals to death is taken for granted. Although Jesus refrained from violence and admonished his followers to "put aside the sword" (Matt 26:52), he did not deny the state has the power to impose the death penalty and, in his interactions with Pontius Pilate, seems to affirm it as a right given by God (John 19:11).

The early Christians evidently had nothing against capital punishment. The Apostle Paul, in an apparent reference to the death penalty, said that a magistrate "does not bear the sword in vain! It is the servant of God to execute wrath on the wrongdoer" (Rom 13:4). Augustine (d. 430), the father of all Western theology, taught that a representative of the state who puts criminals to death according to the rule of law does not violate the commandment "Thou shalt not kill." The great medieval theologian Thomas Aquinas (d. 1274) did not produce a comprehensive treatment of capital punishment, but he did say it is not intrinsically evil and can in certain circumstances be imposed as a last resort to protect the good of the community.

The Catechism of the Council of Trent, published in 1566, taught that God entrusted the power of life and death to civil authorities and the use of this power was not a crime of murder but an act of obedience to the fifth commandment. In modern times, St. John Henry Newman (d. 1890) wrote in a letter to a friend that magistrates have the right to execute criminals and that the Church should sanction its use. Based on evidence from Scripture and tradition, Avery Dulles concluded that it is a "settled point of doctrine" that the state has the authority to impose the death sentence in serious cases.

We should note that Avery Dulles went on to argue that, in the contemporary world, the state should not exercise its right to execute criminals because capital punishment on balance does more harm than good.

Nevertheless, I know from several private conversations with Avery that his passion on this issue was to defend the traditional teaching and maintain doctrinal continuity. Over the years, Dulles came to fear the relativizing of doctrine in the post–Vatican II Church and endeavored to support doctrinal continuity, including maintaining the "settled doctrine" on the right of the state to execute criminals convicted of murder.

Question: What is my reaction to the way Avery Dulles approached the issue of the death penalty?

The Case Against

In his encyclical *Fratelli tutti*, Pope Francis teaches that "the death penalty is 'inadmissible' and the Church is firmly committed to calling for its abolition worldwide" (no. 263). The pope justifies this teaching, stating that "not even a murderer loses his personal dignity and God himself pledges to guarantee this" (no. 269).

This official teaching was the culmination of growing opposition to capital punishment that intensified after the Second Vatican Council, which ended in 1965. During the 1970s, Dorothy Day (d. 1980), founder of the Catholic Worker Movement, consistently spoke out publicly against the death penalty. In his 1995 encyclical, *The Gospel of Life*, Pope John Paul expressed near total opposition to the death penalty, arguing that with modern improvements in penal systems, the need for capital punishment to protect society from criminals is "very, very rare, if not practically non-existent" (no. 56). At the end of his 1999 pastoral visit to the United States, the pope called on Catholics to proclaim the gospel of life by lobbying against the death penalty, which he called "cruel and unnecessary."

The *Catechism of the Catholic Church*, published in 1992, taught that the traditional teaching of the Church "does not exclude recourse to the death penalty" (no. 2267). Under the leadership of Pope Francis, the teaching was revised in 2018 to read in "light of the Gospel," the death penalty is "inadmissible because it is an attack on the inviolability and dignity of the person" (no. 2267). After noting the traditional teaching, the text offers reasons for the revisions. There is today an increasing awareness that the dignity of the person is not lost even after the commission of very serious crimes. Furthermore, states have developed more effective systems of detention that "ensure due protection of citizens" without definitively depriving the guilty "of the possibility of redemption." We should note that the fundamental basis for the change of doctrine is the "dignity of the human person" now better understood in the light of the Gospel. In explaining the revision, the Vatican insisted that it "expressed an authentic development of doctrine that is not in contradiction with the previous teaching of the Magisterium."

In *Fratelli tutti*, Pope Francis expanded on his rejection of the death penalty. He cites Pope Nicholas I (d. 867), who declared efforts should be made to "free from the punishment of death not only each of the innocent, but all the guilty as well" (no. 265). He also referred to the great theologian St. Augustine (d. 430) who, in a trial of a murderer who killed two priests, pleaded with the judge: "Don't let the atrocity of their sins feed a desire for vengeance, but desire instead to heal the wounds which theses deeds have inflicted on their souls" (no. 265). Following Augustine, Francis argued that the death penalty not only can fuel vengeance but also rules out the possibility of conversion.

Among the many arguments against the death penalty, Pope Francis called attention to the "possibility of judicial error." In this regard, a 2021 study by the Death Penalty Information Center showed that of the last 1,500 U.S. citizens executed, at least 185 were exonerated posthumously. Noting that the death penalty can be used to persecute minorities, the pope went on to urge all Christians and people of good will to work for the abolition of the death penalty (no. 268). In his monthly prayer intention for September 2022, Pope Francis revisited his major objections to the death penalty, which "offers no justice to victims, but encourages revenge." It is morally wrong because it violates human dignity and destroys life, the most important gift we have received. The pope senses a growing "No" around the world to capital punishment that he sees as "a great sign of hope." Finally, Pope Francis invites us to pray that the death penalty may be legally abolished in every country.

Question: What do I make of the case against capital punishment outlined by Pope Francis?

10

IMMIGRATION

Wise Guidance from Pope Francis

The British biographer of Pope Francis, Austen Ivereigh, published an article in the March 2023 issue of *Commonweal* entitled "From Strangers to Siblings," arguing that Francis has put immigration at the center of his Petrine ministry, acting as the greatest advocate for migrants and refugees on the world stage. As a son of Italian immigrants who moved to Buenos Aires in the 1930s, he has firsthand knowledge of the challenges facing immigrants; as the head of a world church, he is well aware of the enormity of the current crisis, with some 70 million persons seeking a new home; and as a moral leader, Francis recognizes that immigration presents the great challenge of our time to heed the call of Christ to be merciful to the stranger.

After his election as pope in 2013, Francis made his first visit outside Rome to the tiny island of Lampedusa off the coast of Sicily, where he honored immigrants from Africa who died crossing the Mediterranean trying to find a better life in Europe. In 2018, Francis visited a squalid refugee camp in Lesbos, Greece, where he befriended a family of Syrian refugees and flew them and nine other Muslim refugees on the papal plane to Rome, where they have been helped to build a new life. When the pope visited Mexico and the United States in 2016, he celebrated Mass near the southern border, where he called forced migration a "human tragedy" and lauded "prophets of mercy" who are on the front lines accompanying migrants. In his homily, he identified poverty, violence, and drug trafficking as root causes of migration from Central America to the United States. He concluded his homily on a hopeful note: there is still a "way out" and "time to implore the mercy of God."[1]

In *Fratelli tutti*, Pope Francis invites Christians to reflect on the immigration crisis in light of the parable of the Good Samaritan (Luke 10:25–37). In the parable, the priest and Levite, on the one hand, who held prominent social positions, did not take time to notice or help the injured man. On the other hand, the Samaritan, a despised unclean foreigner, put aside his own needs and desires and gave his time and money to care for the victim, a stranger. At this point in his exposition of the parable, Pope Francis directs us to the Gospel of Matthew, where Jesus says, "I was a stranger and you welcomed me" (25:35). When we welcome uprooted immigrants today, we are welcoming Christ himself (cf. no. 84).

In a section of *Fratelli tutti* on "Borders and Their Limits," Pope Francis argues that persons who are living in countries where a dignified life is impossible have a right to seek a home where they can meet the basic needs of their families and find personal fulfillment. Given this right, Francis contends that the world needs developed countries that can "welcome, protect, promote, and integrate immigrants," while preserving their own cultural and religious identity (no. 129). The pope offers some concrete proposals for integrating migrants: simplify granting of visas; provide equitable access to the justice system and educational opportunities; and expand the possibility of employment (cf. no. 131). Citing the example of Latino immigration to the United States, Francis insists that the process can be mutually enriching as both cultures expand their outlook and learn from each other (cf. no. 134). Finally, amid the "dark clouds" that hover over the immigration crisis, Pope Francis urges us to advance along "new paths of hope" that lift our spirits and alert us to the seeds of goodness, truth, justice and love that God continues to sow in our human family (nos. 54–55).

Question: What aspect of the teaching of Pope Francis is most interesting?

Should There Be a Path to Citizenship?

According to a 2023 Pew Research Study, by the end of 2021 the unauthorized immigrant population in the United States reached 10.5 million, about 5 million of whom are considered "essential workers," employed in health care, farming, food production, and distribution.

Immigration

As a nation, we are faced with serious challenges to our immigration policies, including whether unauthorized immigrants should be given a path to citizenship that would allow them to vote, receive government benefits such as social security, and bring family members living abroad to join them in the United States. This process should be distinguished from "legalization" that would allow them to earn a green card enabling them to work in the United States and travel in and out of the country, but would not grant them the right to vote. Unauthorized immigrants include the so-called Dreamers, who were brought to the United States as children and have attended school here and typically identify as Americans, but do not have social security numbers, preventing them from getting a driver's license and applying for college. According to one estimate, there are 2.3 million Dreamers now in the United States, about one-fifth of the total undocumented population.

According to ProCon.org, a nonprofit charitable organization, one of the main arguments against a path to citizenship (or "amnesty" as opponents commonly call it) is that it rewards immigrants who broke the law at the expense of those who entered the country legally. It also incentivizes other unwary immigrants to pursue illegal means, often engaging drug cartels and smugglers to take them on expensive and dangerous journeys to get them across the border, where they are told they will be safe and secure.

Proponents, however, argue that immigrants who have lived in the country for years, paying taxes and contributing to the well-being of the country, deserve the opportunity to follow the proper legal procedures to attain the great blessing of citizenship. This will help stabilize their families and make them even more productive members of society. Offering this legal path is in accord with our history as a nation of immigrants as well as a nation of laws. In short, a path to citizenship would provide relief and security for immigrant families while bringing many needed benefits to the country.

The United States Conference of Catholic Bishops (USCCB) has long supported legislation that provides immigrants with a pathway to citizenship in the United States. For example, in a 2013 statement, the bishops urged Congress to pass legislation that would allow "foreign nationals of good character to obtain lawful permanent residence with an eventual path to citizenship."[2] In a 2021 statement, the bishops said: "We cannot persist in relegating these members of our society to the margins, especially when we simultaneously depend on so many of them for our collective well-being."[3] And in 2022, the USCCB urged Congress to pass legislation that would provide all Dreamers with a path to citizenship, a "permanent solution" that is just, compassionate, and beneficial to both new immigrants and American citizens.[4]

Question: What is my position on providing a path to citizenship?

The Role of the Parish

Historically, Catholic parishes in the United States have played a prominent role in helping the millions of European Catholic immigrants who came to America before 1924 to overcome nativist prejudice and make it socially, economically, and politically in their new country. In their 2000 pastoral letter, "Welcoming the Stranger among Us," the American bishops confessed that too often our parishes have not done as well in meeting the spiritual and institutional needs of the new largely Hispanic immigrants. They suggest ways to improve parish ministry to the new immigrants: respect their rich diverse cultures; incorporate their distinctive liturgical and devotional practices into the prayer life of the parish; draw on diocesan and community resources to help immigrants meet their social, economic, legal, and educational needs; pay special attention to young immigrants who often feel a tension between the traditional culture of their parents and the new American way of life; and work in solidarity with community organizers to empower the new immigrants to find their own way to live as productive, happy citizens of their new country.

Among the many Catholic parishes providing excellent pastoral ministry for new immigrants, we raise up St. Adalbert Parish in South Bend, Indiana. The parish was founded in 1910 to serve the large influx of Polish immigrants who settled in the South Bend area. Today it serves around one thousand families, of which 90 percent are Hispanic. The parish grade school is dedicated to meeting the needs of its almost entirely Hispanic student body. The parish extends its ministry to the Hispanic community by partnering with a local community center known as La Casa, a secular nonprofit organization that maintains a close relationship with the parish. For youth, the center provides after-school programs to help them keep up academically and master virtual learning opportunities. For adults, it offers classes to learn the English language and to navigate the path to citizenship that includes passing the required exams.

The parish hosts "Know Your Rights" sessions put on by La Casa to help immigrant families understand their legal options and how to interact with law enforcement. It also hosts meetings of the local Faith in Action group that promotes faith-based organizing to secure justice for immigrant communities. For instance, Faith in Action succeeded in getting the city of South Bend to issue municipal IDs to immigrants who are unable to get official federal IDs so that they can access local banks, schools, and government offices. Faith in Action went on to work with others to extend this ID initiative to the state level.

The outstanding ministry of St. Adalbert Parish to new Hispanic immigrants provides concrete examples of proposals made by the U.S. bishops. It is especially helpful in demonstrating the importance of partnering with other agencies such as community organizations and faith-based advocacy groups.

Question: How can my parish improve its ministry to new immigrants?

The U.S. Economy

In July 2016, when Donald Trump accepted the Republican nomination for president, he claimed: "Decades of record immigration have provided lower wages and higher unemployment for citizens, especially African-American and Latino workers."[5] Trump was citing research by Harvard economist George Borjas, who said Trump did accurately portray one part of his findings—that the recent large influx of immigrants has reduced the annual wages of agricultural and service workers. However, Borjas accused Trump of ignoring his broader conclusion that immigration is a net good for the nation, increasing the total wealth of the whole population. Nevertheless, Trump and his followers have continued to propagate this misleading citation of scholarly research in his anti-immigrant rhetoric.

MEDITATIONS ON CATHOLIC SOCIAL TEACHING

Testifying before Congress on September 20, 2023, the American Immigration Council, a nonprofit advocacy group, insisted that solid research demonstrates that immigrants of all types—low-skilled, high-skilled, undocumented, humanitarian, family-based, and employment-based—contribute substantially to the U.S. economy, help power our growth, and provide an overall net financial benefit to this country. Even those who come to the United States through purely humanitarian channels will, over time, pay more into the system than they draw from it. For example, in 2019, immigrant households collectively earned $1.7 trillion in income and paid $467 billion in taxes. Despite being 13.6 percent of the total U.S. population, immigrants make up 26.1 percent of agriculture workers and 45 percent of all people employed in the meatpacking industry. The congressional testimony of the American Immigration Council concluded that, without robust immigration, "America's food producers would see even greater labor shortages and American consumers would pay even higher prices for everyday food items." In this regard, the Brookings Institute published a report in 2024 arguing that, commencing in 2022, the massive influx of immigrants enabled the U.S. economy to grow without causing uncontrollable inflation and without causing the recession predicted by most economists.

Drawing on Catholic Social Teaching, the American bishops have consistently advocated for policies that would allow more immigrant workers to enter the country. For example, in their 2013 statement "Catholic Church's Position on Immigration Reform," the bishops noted that over the last several decades the demand of U.S. businesses for low-skilled workers has "grown exponentially" while the supply of such workers has diminished.[6] At that time, there were only five thousand green cards available annually to allow low-skilled workers to enter the country lawfully to reside and work. In this situation, the bishops noted that CST insists that prosperous nations have a special obligation to welcome foreigners seeking "means of livelihood" not available in their homeland. According to the U.S. bishops, any program should include workplace protections, living wage levels, safeguards against displacement of U.S. workers, and family unity.[7] In 2024, the USCCB continued to lobby Congress for expanded access to work authorization within a comprehensive employment-based immigration plan.

As we ponder the impact of immigration on the U.S. economy, we do well to recall relevant CST themes. Immigrants are members of God's family, human persons redeemed by Christ, individuals with inherent dignity worthy of respect. The opportunity for them to work enables them to participate in God's ongoing creation, to develop and fulfill their God-given gifts and talents, and to know the satisfaction of providing a living for their families. Our Christian faith assures us that when we help an immigrant, we help Christ himself.

Question: For me, what is the most compelling argument supporting my view on immigration and the economy?

Refugees Seeking Asylum

According to a United Nations report, by the end of 2022 there were over 108 million refugees displaced worldwide by violence, social conflict, and persecution due to their race, religion, nationality, political opinions, or membership in a particular social group.[8] Almost 768,000 refugees sought asylum in the United States between 1990 and 2021, some for what is known as "affirmative asylum," which grants permanent asylum status, and others for "defensive asylum" to avoid deportation by a "standard removal" proceeding already in progress.

Individuals seeking asylum all have their own personal story that involves serious threats and hope for a safer future. A Venezuelan woman named Yomardy shared her story of the happy life she once had in her beautiful native country, surrounded by kind people and blessed with a celebrated career as an award-winning teacher, an achievement that won her a prestigious American scholarship. While in the United States, she spoke out against the corruption of the Venezuelan government that has led to food shortages, high unemployment, unchecked violence, and the highest crime rate in the world. The Venezuelan government responded by branding her an "enemy of the state," making it extremely dangerous for her to return to Venezuela. Warned by her mother not to come home, Yomardy applied for asylum in the United States, delaying her dream to use her enhanced expertise to work for governmental reforms in her homeland.

The process of gaining asylum in the United States is complicated, lengthy, and stressful. The U.S. government has specific requirements for those seeking asylum: be present in the United States; apply within one year of last arrival; get fingerprinted and pass background security checks; and interview with an asylum official who will render a decision. In 2022, this process took about six years to complete and only about 20 percent of applicants were successful.

In 2017, the American bishops issued a statement supporting a process that allows everyone who is seeking asylum to have their cases heard expeditiously and judged fairly. The bishops also called on the U.S. government to respect the international law that prohibits returning a refugee to a country where they are at risk of persecution, torture, and death.[9]

In May 2023, President Biden instituted an "asylum travel ban" that prevents refugees from seeking asylum in the United States if they passed through other countries on their way to the United States. In response, Bishop Mark Seitz, spokesperson for the USCCB on immigration, published an article in the May 2023 issue of *America* magazine, decrying this policy as "indefensibly regressive," and claiming that it further diminished the "rights of vulnerable persons on the move at the border" who would be in danger of exploitation by drug cartels and traffickers. The bishop went on to call for a culture of "renewed solidarity and hospitality" that would treat asylum seekers with compassion and respect.[10]

Question: What is my opinion of U.S. policy on asylum seekers?

The Impact on Culture

When Donald Trump began his campaign for president in 2016, he accused Mexico of sending its criminals, drug dealers, and rapists to the United States. Since then, he has continued his anti-immigrant rhetoric, insisting that illegal immigrants "coming from prisons, from mental institutions from all over the world" are "poisoning the blood of our nation."[11] Critics have noted that the term "blood poisoning" was used by Hitler in *Mein Kampf* to identify the cause of the demise of all great cultures in the past. Trump has consistently called the influx of immigrants an "invasion," suggesting it as an attack on our American way of life and has even claimed that undocumented immigrants are "not humans" but "animals."[12]

Immigration

White supremacists typically describe immigration in apocalyptic terms as an ultimate life and death struggle to maintain the American way of life. For instance, David Duke, the former head of the Ku Klux Klan, declared that "massive immigration threatens the continued existence of our very genotype" and "our way of life in the United States." Duke also claimed that Mexico and other third-world countries are "dumping their chaff onto American shores" that sounds a "funeral dirge of the America we love."[13]

Many prominent immigrants, however, have made positive contributions to American culture. For example, Frank Capra (1897–1991), an Italian Catholic immigrant, made an impact on the movie industry with films such as *It's a Wonderful Life* (1947) that highlighted the decency of the common American. Albert Einstein (1879–1955), a Jewish refugee from Nazi Germany, forever changed the way we understand space and time and encouraged many young American scientists to pursue careers in quantum studies.

Many immigrants from Latin America have become stars in American Major League Baseball, most prominently Miguel Cabrera, one of the greatest hitters in the history of the game. Born in Venezuela, Cabrera came to the United States in 2003 at the age of twenty, playing five seasons with the Florida Marlins and sixteen with the Detroit Tigers, where he made his home and contributed to the community through his foundation that has helped many kids to achieve their dreams. Miguel, who always played the game with youthful enthusiasm and a playful spirit, often bantering with players and fans, serves as a reminder to our commercialized sports culture that athletic sports are a form of leisure activity with intrinsic value that should be fun and uplifting.

Noting these celebrated immigrants invites us to recall the many unsung immigrants who have significantly enriched our national culture by sacrificing so that their children could receive a good education while adding diversity to our school system, participating in the political process that strengthens our democracy, being good neighbors who foster a sense of community, and practicing their faith tradition that enhances the moral fiber of our culture.

In his encyclical *Fratelli tutti*, Pope Francis argues that immigration can be mutually beneficial, enriching both cultures (nos. 129–53). The pope invites us to see an encounter between two cultures as a "gift exchange." Noting that nations are always at risk of succumbing to "cultural sclerosis," the pope urges us to "open our hearts to those who are different" and to see "differences" as an opportunity to grow in mutual respect (no. 134). A country that welcomes immigrants while remaining solidly grounded in its original cultural tradition is "a treasure for the whole of humanity" (no. 137).

Question: Do I think immigration harms or helps American culture?

11

WAR AND PEACE

The Just War Tradition

In Catholic Social Teaching there are two general approaches to the morality of war: pacifism, which opposes all war, and the just war tradition, which provides criteria for determining whether a specific war can be morally justified or not. In recent years, under the leadership of Pope Francis, the Catholic Church has emphasized pacifism so strongly that the possibility of a just war is now practically impossible to imagine. In the May 2023 issue of *Commonweal*, the moral theologian Tobias Winright published the article "The Possibility of a Just War," arguing that the war in Ukraine has moved some Catholic scholars to recognize that we have acted prematurely in "relegating the just war tradition to the margins or even supplanting it with pacifism."[1] To make his point, Winright invites us to reflect on a young Ukrainian soldier bravely defending his country from an unjust attack. With the just war criteria in mind, we can see his service not as failed pacifism but as participation in a just war defending his country.

Winright cites theologian Massimo Faggioli and Cardinal Robert McElroy in suggesting that the Ukraine war might be a "turning point" in Catholic teaching on war and peace, with renewed emphasis on the contemporary relevance of the just war criteria. Both Faggioli and McElroy lauded the U.S. bishops' 1983 pastoral letter, *The Challenge of Peace*, that made good use of the traditional just war criteria, including last resort, just cause, and proportionality (that is, where more good than harm is accomplished).

Along this same line, Winright cites journalist Michael Sean Winters writing in the *National Catholic Reporter* that the "most significant intellectual development" in the Church in 2022 was the "emphatic rein-statement of just war theory as the principle Catholic moral approach to violence."[2]

In support of this view, Tobias Winright cites neoconservative scholar George Weigel, who maintains that the just war tradition is the "normative" way of thinking about war and peace in the classic Catholic approach to international relations. Applying this approach, Weigel holds that Russia's war on Ukraine is clearly unjustified and unjustly conducted, while Ukraine is engaged in a war of legitimate self-defense "conducted proportionately and discriminately."[3]

Winright also finds support in Villanova professor George Beyer, who abhors war and opposed the U.S. wars in Afghanistan and Iraq but supports Ukraine's military action because the Russian invasion is about "annihilating" a country and its citizens and opening the door to further Russian expansionism. While Beyer supports active nonviolence and peacemaking priorities, he is convinced that these alone will not stop the "Russian juggernaut." In this situation, the evil is so great that a defensive war is justified to prevent "grave atrocities on a massive scale."[4]

In summary, Tobias Winright has assembled an impressive group of scholars to support his claim that the Ukraine war has highlighted the relevance of the traditional just war criteria for judging the morality of some wars today.

Question: What is my opinion of the just war tradition?

Christian Pacifism

In the early Church, there was a strong movement toward Christian pacificism, based on the teaching of Jesus in the Gospel of Matthew: "Put your sword back into its place; for all who take the sword will perish by the sword" (26:52); "But if anyone strikes you on the right cheek, turn the other also" (5:39); "You have heard that it was said, 'You shall love your neighbor and hate your enemy,' but I say to you, love your enemies and pray for those who persecute you" (5:43–44); "Blessed are the pure in heart, for they will see God" (5:8).

In the first centuries of the Christian era, some followers of Jesus refused to serve in the Roman army and were martyred for their civil disobedience. Important early scholars, including Origen (d. 254), Tertullian (d. 220), and Cyprian of Carthage (d. 258), taught that Christians should not fight in the Roman army or engage in violent actions.

Throughout subsequent Christian history, there have been many important witnesses to Christian pacifism. One of the most influential was Francis of Assisi (d. 1226), son of a wealthy Italian merchant, who renounced his privileged life, lived a life of poverty, founded the Franciscan order, and was known for his embrace of lepers and his appreciation of nature. His commitment to gospel nonviolence is represented in the story of his effort to be a peacemaker during the Fifth Crusade to liberate the Holy Land from Muslim control. According to legend, Francis made the hazardous journey to Damietta, Egypt, where a fierce battle was raging, crossed enemy lines with a companion, and was badly beaten. He eventually reached Sultan Malik-al-Kamil and pleaded with him to stop the bloodshed. The Sultan was impressed with Francis and his courage and let him return to the crusader lines without further harm. Francis did not stop the war, but he gave an inspired witness to Christ's call to love our enemies.

Dorothy Day (d. 1980), the founder of the Catholic Worker Movement, was a consistent advocate of Christian pacifism. A month after the bombing of Pearl Harbor, Day wrote in *The Catholic Worker*: "We are still pacifists...we will not participate in armed warfare or in making munitions, or by buying government bonds to prosecute the war, or in urging others to these efforts."[5] In the 1950s during the height of the Cold War, when the state of New York mandated citizens to take cover during civil defense drills, Dorothy Day refused to comply, sitting on a park bench where she was arrested five times and spent some six weeks in jail.

In response to the Ukraine war, William Cavanaugh, professor of Catholic studies at DePaul University, published an article in the May 2023 issue of *Commonweal*, suggesting that nonviolent active resistance to the Russian invasion might have been a better option, since it would have avoided the carnage of war and could have made it impossible for the Russians to control the country of Ukraine.[6]

In this regard, we can recall Erica Chenoweth and Maria Stephan's important book, *Why Civil Resistance Works*, in which they studied over three hundred cases of violent and nonviolent resistance and concluded that, over time, active nonviolence is more effective with less carnage and a better chance of more humane outcomes.[7] Two of the more striking examples of the effectiveness of active nonviolence are Gandhi's liberation of India from British colonial rule and Martin Luther King Jr.'s success in securing civil rights for African Americans.

In his encyclical *Fratelli tutti*, Pope Francis made official his effort to replace reliance on the just war tradition with commitment to Christian pacifism that reflects the teaching of Christ to love our enemies and avoid violence.

Question: What is my opinion of Christian pacifism?

Peacebuilding—A Third Way

In her excellent book *Blessed Are the Peacemakers: Pacifism, Just War, and Peacebuilding*, the respected Catholic moral theologian Lisa Cahill presents an alternative to the just war tradition and Christian pacifism that she names "peacebuilding." This recent approach gives "almost exclusive priority to the positive and nonviolent cultivation of peace" rather than examining exceptional situations where war might be justified.[8] Compared to pacifism, peacebuilding is a movement that seeks partners to "create, highlight, and implement concrete alternatives to violence, strategies that can and do transform situations," leading to a just and peaceful society. Peacebuilding is a "family of practices" that aims to "resolve injustices in nonviolent ways and to transform the structural conditions that generate deadly conflict." Christian peacebuilders join Christian pacifists and just war advocates in sensing the urgency of reducing violence through "practical and flexible initiatives" that they see as integral to Christian discipleship.[9]

Cahill emphasizes that "defeating violence requires flexibility, creativity, pragmatism, and determination." For her, Christian peacebuilding is a "way of yoking gospel nonviolence to effective action for change, despite the morally ambiguous circumstances in which its mission must be embedded." It seeks a long-term and sustainable solution based on addressing the root cause of "pervasive global cycles of conflict."[10]

According to Cahill, peacebuilding highlights the practical, located, pragmatic, and provisional nature of Christian responses to injustice and human suffering. It embraces active hope that those realities can be changed nonviolently. To accomplish this, peacebuilders seek to form "networks and structures of political responsibility" that "expand the scope of justice within local, national, regional, and global institutions."[11]

In her concluding chapter, Cahill summarizes some of her major themes. Peacebuilding starts with the "desire, determination, and courage of people who are willing to take risks." They combine a passion to live in peace with a trust that faithful persons can build a peaceful life together. Peacebuilders empower individuals and communities to name and resist violence. In a spirit of solidarity, they reach out across religious, racial, and cultural divides to empower victims and survivors of violence to take charge of their own lives. They know that peacebuilding must lead to "broad and deep social practices" that promote personal, social, and political reconciliation.[12]

At the same time, we should remember that peacebuilding is always marred by "incompleteness and moral ambiguity" that can involve "irreducible moral dilemmas." For example, even killing an unjust aggressor in a legitimate war of self-defense still involves an offense against the dignity of human persons and that can produce a sense of guilt and remorse. Finally, Cahill calls peacebuilding a "practical strategy of hope," a Christian virtue that sustains us in times of adversity and alerts us to the power of God's grace operating in our midst.[13]

Question: What aspects of peacebuilding are challenging to me?

Moral Arguments for Nuclear Disarmament

In 2022, Archbishop John Wester of Santa Fe, New Mexico, published a pastoral letter, "Living in the Light of Christ's Peace: A Conversation toward Nuclear Disarmament," with the explicit purpose of fostering serious conversations across the nation on abolishing nuclear weapons. Explaining his passion on this issue, the archbishop recalled his 2017 visit to the Peace Memorial Park in Hiroshima, Japan, commemorating the August 6, 1945, bombing when "humans crossed the line into the darkness of the nuclear age," so that we can now kill "billions of people instantly and even destroy the world in a flash."[14]

MEDITATIONS ON CATHOLIC SOCIAL TEACHING

Archbishop Wester praised Pope Francis for leading the Church in a "dramatic shift" from provisional support for a policy of nuclear deterrence to denouncing nuclear weapons as immoral and calling for their complete abolition.[15] While paying tribute to all the victims of the nuclear attack on Japan, Francis declared that the nuclear arms race creates a false sense of security, poisons international relationships, and damages the environment.[16] Finally, in *Fratelli tutti*, Francis argues that the elimination of nuclear weapons is a "moral and humanitarian imperative" (no. 262).

Archbishop Wester places the teachings of Pope Francis in the context of Catholic Social Teaching going back to Pope John XXIII's 1963 encyclical, *Pacem in terris*, which insisted that lasting peace could not be based on the possession of an equal supply of armaments but only on mutual trust. In the pastoral constitution *Gaudium et spes*, Vatican II taught the arms race is an "utterly treacherous trap for humanity" (no. 81) that is especially harmful to the poor. In a 1987 address to the General Assembly of the United Nations, Pope John Paul II called for "a mutual, progressive, and verifiable reduction of armaments," based on ethical choices that will guarantee a lasting peace. Finally, Archbishop Wester cites Pope Benedict XVI's 2006 World Day of Peace message, which called the notion that states need nuclear weapons to maintain peace "not only baneful but also completely fallacious."[17]

After recalling the development of Catholic Social Teaching on nuclear deterrents, Archbishop Wester invites us to reflect on how Jesus practiced nonviolence. When he began his public ministry, Jesus declared, "The kingdom of God has come near; repent, and believe in the good news" (Mark 1:15), inviting his followers to practice nonviolence here and now. In his Sermon on the Mount, he called us to be peacemakers, to reject violence and to love our enemies (Matthew 5–7).

In Luke's Gospel, Jesus travels to Jerusalem by passing through Samaria. He sends his disciples to a Samaritan village to prepare for his coming, but the people did not welcome him. James and John responded by asking Jesus if they should call fire down from heaven to destroy them, but Jesus rebuked them, and they went to another village (Luke 9:51–56).

When Jesus reached Jerusalem, he took nonviolent, direct action to confront systemic injustice in the temple (Mark 11:15–18). Soon after, Jesus was arrested in the Garden of Gethsemane, and Peter used his sword to defend Jesus, which prompted the Lord to utter his last words to his disciples: "Put your sword back into its place" (Matt 26:52). Archbishop Wester concludes his portrayal of Jesus as a nonviolent peacemaker by noting that he maintained his nonviolent approach throughout his trial, torture, and execution, even forgiving his executioners (Luke 23:34). Furthermore, after his resurrection, he offered a greeting of peace to his disciples who had abandoned him and sent them out to continue his mission of peace and nonviolence, a mission shared by all Christians today in a world threatened by nuclear weapons (John 20:19–23).

Question: How do I react to Archbishop John Wester's moral arguments?

Practical Arguments for Nuclear Disarmament

After presenting moral arguments for nuclear disarmament in "Living in the Light of Christ's Peace," Archbishop Wester went on to present more practical reasons for abolishing nuclear weapons. In the same pastoral letter, Wester noted the world has more than thirteen thousand nuclear weapons, some of them one hundred times more powerful than the two bombs the United States dropped on Japan in August 1945. An estimated twelve thousand U.S., Russian, British, and French warheads remain ready to fire on short notice. The archbishop makes the case that we are now in a new arms race. The United States, which has 3,750 nuclear weapons in its active stockpile, plans to invest $1.7 trillion in modernization over the next thirty years. Russia is also engaged in a major modernization of its nuclear arsenal. China is building hundreds of new hardened silos for intercontinental ballistic missiles with nuclear warheads. The United Kingdom and Pakistan are numerically expanding their nuclear arsenals. Iran has enriched uranium almost to bomb-making capacity. Israel, which is known to have a stockpile of nuclear weapons, has repeatedly threatened preemptive military action against Iran. North Korea has an estimated forty-five nuclear weapons and continues to develop missile delivery systems. According to Wester, this second nuclear arms race is more dangerous than the first, because more countries have them, and terrorists can get hold of them.

In the third and final part of his pastoral letter, Archbishop Wester discusses the failure of nations to abide by the 1970 Non-proliferation Treaty (NPT) signed by 190 countries that involved a "grand bargain," stating that those without nuclear weapons would not seek them while the five nuclear countries—United States, Russia, United Kingdom, France, and China—would also look for ways to stop the arms race and promote nuclear disarmament.[18] In 2014, the Vatican reminded world leaders that the NPT is a "moral commitment" on which the future of the world depends. In his pastoral letter, Wester lamented that more than a half-century after the NPT was signed, the nuclear states have failed to honor the treaty and have, unfortunately, implemented massive nuclear modernization programs.

Turning his attention to the 2017 Treaty on the Prohibition of Nuclear Weapons (TNPW), the archbishop notes that Pope Francis supported the treaty as a "decisive step along the road toward a world without nuclear weapons," which is "not beyond reach," a position Wester supports and actively promotes.[19]

Near the end of his pastoral letter, Wester affirms the Vatican II teaching that the nuclear arms race is a "treacherous trap" that injures the poor to an "intolerable degree" (GS 81). He also appropriated the message of Pope Francis, who after his 2019 pilgrimage to Nagasaki, Japan, insisted that the nuclear arms race squanders resources that could be used to help the millions of families living in poverty. Finally, Archbishop Wester concludes his widely welcomed pastoral letter with an urgent plea: "It is time to take up the hard work of nuclear disarmament and move toward the creation and building of a new culture of justice that cares for our planet and offers peace for everyone."[20]

Question: How can I participate in the conversation on nuclear disarmament?

EPILOGUE

This book demonstrates the dynamic character of Catholic Social Teaching that has developed as the Christian community comes to a deeper understanding of the example and teaching of Christ and applies it to evolving situations in the world. With the decision of Pope Francis to focus on synodality as the primary means to renew the Church, CST is poised to reveal even more of its treasure. Synodality calls Catholics to develop habits of ecclesial discernment that will enable the church to function more globally. We will hear more of the concerns of people on the margins and their witness to the transforming power of the gospel. Catholic Social Teaching is a dynamic, evolving treasure that will help us navigate the challenges that await us in a spirit of hope.

NOTES

Part I: THE DOCUMENTS
1. Papal and Conciliar Documents

1. See Charles Curran, *Catholic Social Teaching: A Historical, Theological and Ethical Analysis* (Washington, DC: Georgetown University Press, 2002).

2. Marvin Krier Mich, *Catholic Social Teaching and Movements* (Mystic, CT: Twenty-Third Publications, 1994), 3–29.

3. Mich, *Catholic Social Teaching*, 15.

4. Mich, *Catholic Social Teaching*, 17.

5. Mich, *Catholic Social Teaching*, 18.

6. From Richard John Neuhaus, Op-Ed, *Wall Street Journal*, May 1, 1991, cited in Acton Staff, "Initial Reactions to Centesimus Annus," *Religion and Liberty* 1, no. 3 (2010), www.acton.org/pub/religion-liberty/volume-1-number-3/initial-reactions-centesimus-annus.

7. From Michael Novak, Editorial, *Washington Post*, May 7, 2010, cited in Acton Staff, "Initial Reactions to Centesimus Annus," *Religion and Liberty* 1, no. 3 (2010).

8. Kenneth R. Himes, ed., *Modern Catholic Social Teaching: Commentaries and Interpretations* (Washington, DC: Georgetown University Press, 2005), 507.

9. Stacy Meichtry, "Pope Calls for a Group to Oversee World Markets," *Wall Street Journal*, July 8, 2009.

10. Republic Title, "History of Earth Day," *Republic Title*, April 22, 2024, www.republictitle.com/earth-day.

11. Quoted in "At First, I Thought I Was Fighting to Save Rubber Trees. Now I Realize I Am Fighting for Humanity: The Fortieth Newsletter

(2019)," Tricontinental.org, October 3, 2019, thetricontinental.org/newsletterissue/at-first-i-thought-i-was-fighting-to-save-rubber-trees-now-i-realize-i-am-fighting-for-humanity-the-fortieth-newsletter-2019.

12. Most Reverend Robert W. McElroy, "Paradise Lost: The Urgent Summons of *Laudato Si'* to the American People at This Moment in Our History," *Journal of Moral Theology* 9 Special Issue 1 (2020): 30–38.

13. "Video Message of the Holy Father on the Occasion of the Launch of the Laudato si' Action Platform," May 25, 2021, press.vatican.va/content/salastampa/en/bollettino/pubblico/2021/05/25/210525c.html.

2. The Seven Themes of Catholic Social Teaching

1. Anna Rowlands, *Toward a Politics of Communion: Catholic Social Teaching in Dark Times* (London: Bloomsbury, 2021).

2. Rowlands, *Toward a Politics of Communion*, 93–109.

3. Rowlands, *Toward a Politics of Communion*, 177–214.

4. Rowlands, *Toward a Politics of Communion*, 269–92.

5. Rowlands, *Toward a Politics of Communion*, 239–67.

6. Rowlands, *Toward a Politics of Communion*, 269–91, at 269.

7. Rowlands, *Toward a Politics of Communion*, 279–80.

3. Pastoral Letters and Statements of the U.S. Catholic Bishops

1. See also John Paul II, "Address to the International Conference on Nutrition," *Origins* 22, no. 28 (December 24, 1992): 475.

2. See also John Paul II, "Address to the Diplomatic Corps, January 16, 1993," *Origins* 22, no. 34 (February 4, 1993): 587.

3. "Editorial: Bishops' Pastoral Letter on Racism Lacks Sustained Urgency," *National Catholic Reporter*, November 19, 2018, www.ncronline.org/opinion/editorial/editorial-bishops-pastoral-letter-racism-lacks-sustained-urgency.

4. Daniel P. Horan, "The Bishops' Letter Fails to Recognize That Racism Is a White Problem," *National Catholic Reporter*, February 20, 2019, www.ncronline.org/opinion/faith-seeking-understanding/bishops-letter-fails-recognize-racism-white-problem.

Part II: MEDITATIONS ON CATHOLIC SOCIAL TEACHING
4. Euthanasia

1. Pope Francis, "Pope Francis: The Dying Need Palliative Care, Not Euthanasia or Assisted Suicide," General Audience, February 9, 2022, www.vatican.va/content/francesco/en/audiences/2022/documents/20220209-udienza-generale.html.

5. Abortion

1. See *Epistle of Barnabas* 19 (AD 74).

2. John Calvin, *Harmony of the Law*, vol. III under the sixth commandment, political supplements (referencing Exod 21:22).

3. Garry Wills, "The Bishops Are Wrong about Biden—and Abortion," *New York Times*, June 27, 2021, www.nytimes.com/2021/06/27/opinion/biden-bishops-communion-abortion.html.

4. Alexandra DeSanctis, "Garry Wills Is Wrong about the Bishops and Abortion," *National Review*, June 28, 2021, www.nationalreview.com/corner/garry-wills-is-wrong-about-the-bishops-and-abortion.

5. For the quotes from Cardinal McElroy, see J. D. Flynn, "The 'Message' of McElroy's Red Hat," *The Pillar*, May 29, 2022, www.pillarcatholic.com/p/the-message-of-mcelroys-red-hat.

6. Mary Gordon, "This Pregnancy: Each One Is Different," *Commonweal*, November 1, 2022, www.commonwealmagazine.org/pregnancy.

7. Carol Gilligan, *In a Different Voice: Psychological Theory and Women's Development* (Cambridge, MA: Harvard University Press, 2016).

8. Richard McCormick, *How Brave a New World: Dilemmas in Bioethics* (New York: Doubleday, 1981), 176–87.

9. United States Conference of Catholic Bishops, "USCCB Statement on U.S. Supreme Court Ruling in *Dobbs v. Jackson*," June 24, 2022, www.usccb.org/news/2022/usccb-statement-us-supreme-court-ruling -dobbs-v-jackson.

10. Cathleen Kaveny, "Deepening the Division: Why Alito Should Have Listened to Roberts," *Commonweal*, September 25, 2022, https:// www.commonwealmagazine.org/deepening-divisions.

11. Archbishop Gomez, "USCCB President's Statement on the Inauguration of Joseph R. Biden, Jr., as 46th President of the United States of America," January 20, 2021, www.usccb.org/news/2021/usccb -presidents-statement-inauguration-joseph-r-biden-jr-46th-president -united-states.

12. Eric Bradner, "Joe Biden Was Denied Communion at Catholic Church in South Carolina," CNN, October 29, 2019, www.cnn.com/ 2019/10/29/politics/joe-biden-denied-communion-south-carolina -catholic-church/index.html.

13. "Chaput Says Denying Biden Communion Is 'Pastoral' Not 'Political,'" *Catholic News Agency*, December 4, 2020, www .catholicnewsagency.com/news/46807/chaput-says-denying-biden -communion-is-pastoral-not-political.

14. Julie Asher, "Archbishop Cordileone Says No Communion for Speaker Pelosi over Position on Abortion," *National Catholic Reporter*, May 20, 2022, www.ncronline.org/news/people/archbishop-cordileone -says-no-communion-speaker-pelosi-over-position-abortion.

15. Francis X. Rocca, "Catholic Bishops Debate Communion for Biden, Politicians Who Support Abortion Rights," *Wall Street Journal*, June 17, 2021, www.wsj.com/articles/catholic-bishops-debate-com munion-for-biden-11623937299.

16. Tracy Wilkinson, "Pope Francis Is a Biden Fan, but Some U.S. Catholic Leaders Give President a Frosty Reception," *Los Angeles Times*, February 3, 2021, www.latimes.com/politics/story/2021-02-03/u -s-catholic-group-giving-biden-a-surprisingly-frosty-reception.

17. "Bishop Asks for Prayers for New President and Vice President, Calls for Dialogue and Collaboration," *San Diego Catholic*, January

20, 2021, sdcatholic.org/news-release/bishop-asks-for-prayers-for-new
-president-and-vice-president-calls-for-dialogue-and-collaboration.

18. Mark Pattison, "Bishop Warns against 'Weaponization of
Eucharist' with Elected Officials," *National Catholic Reporter*, February
2, 2021, www.ncronline.org/news/bishop-warns-against-weaponization
-eucharist-elected-officials.

6. Caring for Creation

1. Pope Francis, "Video Message of His Holiness Pope Francis
to Mark the Launch of the 'Laudato Si' Action Plan,'" May 28, 2021,
www.vatican.va/content/francesco/en/messages/pont-messages/2021/
documents/papa-francesco_20210525_videomessaggio-laudatosi.html.

2. Lydia O'Kane, "Pope Francis: Care for Water Is Urgent Imperative," *Vatican News*, September 1, 2018, www.vaticannews.va/en/pope/
news/2018-09/pope-francis-care-for-water-is-urgent-imperative.html.

3. United Nations Climate Change, "What Is the Triple Planetary
Crisis?," April 13, 2022, unfccc.int/news/what-is-the-triple-planetary
-crisis.

4. Pope Francis, "Message of the Holy Father Francis for the Celebration of the World Day of Prayer for the Care of Creation," July 21,
2022, press.vatican.va/content/salastampa/en/bollettino/pubblico/2022/
07/21/220721c.html.

5. United Nations Climate Change, "What Is the Triple Planetary
Crisis?," April 13, 2022.

6. General Motors News Release Details, "General Motors, the
Largest U.S. Automaker, Plans to Be Carbon Neutral by 2040," January
28, 2021, investor.gm.com/news-releases/news-release-details/general
-motors-largest-us-automaker-plans-be-carbon-neutral-2040.

7. This saying has been attributed to St. Augustine of Hippo.

7. Humanizing Work

1. See, for example, Pope Francis, "Catechesis of His Holiness for
All Workers of Mercy and Volunteers," Extraordinary Jubilee of Mercy,
September 3, 2016, www.vatican.va/content/francesco/en/speeches/2016/

september/documents/papa-francesco_20160903_giubileo-operatori
-misericordia.html.

2. Benedict Mayaki, "Pope: Volunteers Are the Strength of the Church," *Vatican News*, December 5, 2022, https://www.vaticannews .va/en/pope/news/2022-12/pope-francis-volunteers-volunteering-world -day-video-message.html.

8. Overcoming Racism

1. Pope Francis, "Visit to the Joint Session of the United States Congress," September 24, 2015, www.vatican.va/content/francesco/en/ speeches/2015/september/documents/papa-francesco_20150924_usa -us-congress.html.

10. Immigration

1. Pope Francis, "Homily during Apostolic Journey of His Holiness Pope Francis to Mexico, Ciudad Juárez Fair Grounds," February 17, 2016, www.vatican.va/content/francesco/en/homilies/2016/documents/ papa-francesco_20160217_omelia-messico-ciudad-jaurez.html.

2. Migration and Refugee Services/Office of Migration Policy and Public Affairs, "Catholic Church's Position on Immigration Reform," USCCB, August 2013, www.usccb.org/issues-and-action/human-life -and-dignity/immigration/churchteachingonimmigrationreform.

3. Committee on Migration, "U.S. Bishops' Migration Chairman Commends Inclusion of Legalization Provisions in House Judiciary Committee Reconciliation Measure," USCCB, September 15, 2021, www.usccb.org/news/2021/us-bishops-migration-chairman-commends -inclusion-legalization-provisions-house-judiciary.

4. Committee on Migration, "Following Court Decision on DACA, U.S. Bishops' Migration Chairman Renews Plea for Congress to Provide Legislative Solution," USCCB, October 6, 2022, www.usccb .org/news/2022/following-court-decision-daca-us-bishops-migration -chairman-renews-plea-congress-provide.

5. Donald Trump, "Donald Trump 2016 RNC Draft Speech Transcript," *Politico*, July 21, 2016, www.politico.com/story/2016/07/

full-transcript-donald-trump-nomination-acceptance-speech-at-rnc
-225974.

6. Migration and Refugee Services, "Catholic Church's Position
on Immigration Reform."

7. Migration and Refugee Services, "Catholic Church's Position
on Immigration Reform."

8. USA for UNHCR, "Refugee Statistics," www.unrefugees.org/
refugee-facts/statistics.

9. Committee on Migration, "USCCB Committee on Migration
Chair Strongly Opposes Executive Order Because It Harms Vulnerable
Refugee and Immigrant Families," USCCB, February 6, 2017, www.usccb
.org/news/2017/usccb-committee-migration-chair-strongly-opposes
-executive-order-because-it-harms.

10. Mark Seitz, "Bishop Seitz on Biden's New Asylum Policy:
Death Cannot Be the Cost of Our Immigration Laws," *America*, March
14, 2023, www.americamagazine.org/politics-society/2023/03/14/biden
-asylum-immigration-244876.

11. Olivia Alafriz, "'Poisoning the Blood of Our Country': Trump
Delivers Caustic Attack on Immigrants," *Politico*, December 16, 2023,
www.politico.com/news/2023/12/16/trump-immigration-attack
-00132156.

12. See Nathan Layne, Gram Slattery, and Tim Reid, "Trump Calls
Migrants 'Animals,' Intensifying Focus on Illegal Immigration," *Reuters*,
April 3, 2024, www.reuters.com/world/us/trump-expected-highlight
-murder-michigan-woman-immigration-speech-2024-04-02.

13. Anti-Defamation League, "David Duke: In His Own Words,"
2012, www.adl.org/sites/default/files/David-Duke-long-article.pdf.

11. War and Peace

1. Tobias Winright, "The Possibility of a Just War," *Commonweal*,
May 10, 2023, www.commonwealmagazine.org/possibility-just-war.

2. Michael Sean Winters, "2022 Saw Opposition to Pope Francis,
Plus Intellectual and Ecclesial Shifts," *National Catholic Reporter*, December 26, 2022, www.ncronline.org/opinion/ncr-voices/2022-saw-opposi
tion-pope-francis-plus-intellectual-and-ecclesial-shifts.

3. Winright, "The Possibility of a Just War."

4. Winright, "The Possibility of a Just War."

5. Dorothy Day, "Our Country Passes from Undeclared War to Declared War; We Continue Our Christian Pacifist Stand," *The Catholic Worker Movement*, January 1, 1942, catholicworker.org/868-html.

6. William T. Cavanagh, "No War Is Good," *Commonweal*, May 10, 2023, www.commonwealmagazine.org/ukraine-war-francis-non violence-putin-cavanaugh.

7. Erica Chenoweth and Maria J. Stephan, *Why Civil Resistance Works: The Strategic Logic of Nonviolent Conflict* (New York: Columbia University Press, 2012).

8. Lisa Sowle Cahill, *Blessed Are the Peacemakers: Pacifism, Just War, and Peacebuilding* (Minneapolis: Fortress Press, 2019), 1.

9. Cahill, *Blessed Are the Peacemakers*, 2–8.

10. Cahill, *Blessed Are the Peacemakers*, 19–21.

11. Cahill, *Blessed Are the Peacemakers*, 36.

12. Cahill, *Blessed Are the Peacemakers*, 362.

13. Cahill, *Blessed Are the Peacemakers*, 363.

14. Archbishop John C. Wester, Pastoral Letter, "Living in the Light of Christ's Peace: A Conversation toward Nuclear Disarmament," January 11, 2022, 5, files.ecatholic.com/17613/documents/2022/1/220111_ABW _Pastoral_Letter_LivingintheLightofChristsPeace_Official_Reduced.pdf ?t=1641922875000.

15. Wester, "Living in the Light of Christ's Peace," 9.

16. Pope Francis, "Address on Nuclear Weapons," Nagasaki, November 24, 2019, www.vatican.va/content/francesco/en/speeches/ 2019/november/documents/papa-francesco_20191124_messaggio -arminucleari-nagasaki.html.

17. Pope Benedict XVI, 39th World Day of Peace Message, January 1, 2006, www.vatican.va/content/benedict-xvi/en/messages/peace/ documents/hf_ben-xvi_mes_20051213_xxxix-world-day-peace.html.

18. Wester, "Living in the Light of Christ's Peace," 26.

19. Wester, "Living in the Light of Christ's Peace," 27.

20. Wester, "Living in the Light of Christ's Peace," 30.

ANNOTATED BIBLIOGRAPHY

Curran, Charles. *Catholic Social Teaching: A Historical, Theological, and Ethical Analysis*. Washington, DC: Georgetown University Press, 2002.
In this volume, the respected progressive Catholic moral theologian Charles Curran analyzes the methodology employed by Catholic Social Teaching. He sees development from the philosophical natural law approach of *Rerum novarum* to the methodology of the Vatican II document *Gaudium et spes*, which draws more on explicitly Christian resources to ground its moral teaching. Curran's book is an excellent resource for understanding the specific American secular and religious context for receiving CST. In my own commentaries on the U.S. pastoral letters, *The Challenge of Peace* and *Economic Justice for All*, I have drawn heavily on Curran's theological analysis of these documents.

Himes, Kenneth R., ed. *Modern Catholic Social Teaching: Commentaries and Interpretations*. Washington, DC: Georgetown University Press, 2005.
This large volume is a valuable resource, which I used for background in my commentaries on major papal documents. It also has thoughtful essays on the foundations of CST. In his introduction, Kenneth Himes makes the astute observation that CST documents can be more influential when "translated" into educational programs, social movements, and personal acts of charity and justice—an insight that guided my own approach.

Scripture scholar John Donahue, in his contribution, helps us understand the developing role of Scripture in formulating CST. Vatican II, which mandated that moral theology draw more fully on the teaching of the Bible, has borne fruit in postconciliar CST documents that make greater use of scriptural texts, stories, and images which highlight the example and teachings of Christ. For example, Pope Francis in *Fratelli tutti* has a whole chapter on the parable of the Good Samaritan (Luke 10:25–37), a prototype of the fraternity and social friendship that build bridges of love among all. The greater emphasis on Christ and his familiar stories is more likely to engage the attention of Christians today.

Drawing on Vatican II teachings on the active role of the laity in the Church, the outstanding ecclesiologist Richard Gaillardetz (my good friend, who died all too soon in 2023 in his mid-sixties) argues that the whole Christian community participates in the formulation of CST, not simply the hierarchy who pronounce universal moral principles to be applied by Catholic laypersons. Gaillardetz cites passages in Pope Paul VI's apostolic letter, *Octogesima adveniens*, which call on local Christian communities to analyze their own social situation and to draw on the light of the gospel to determine how to put the social teaching of the Church into action. The U.S. bishops put the insights of Vatican II and Pope Paul VI into practice in developing their 1980s pastoral letters, *The Challenge of Peace* and *Economic Justice for All*, which involved extensive listening sessions and public discussions of early drafts.

In the last chapter of *Modern Catholic Social Teaching*, Jesuit scholar John Coleman points out the importance of viewing CST documents in context of theological developments and social movements, a point that inspired the work of Marvin Mich.

Mich, Marvin Krier. *Catholic Social Teaching and Movements*. Mystic, CT: Twenty-Third Publications, 1994.

This book by the late theologian and social activist Marvin Mich (d. 2018) is the best resource we have for understanding the influence secular and religious movements had in the formulation of official CST documents. Prominent reviewers of the book called it a "unique contribution" and "the best available book of its kind." I found Mich's extensive treatment of U.S. theologian John Courtney Murray, SJ, to be especially helpful in understanding Vatican II's teaching on religious freedom.

Pontifical Council for Justice and Peace. *Compendium of the Social Doctrine of the Church*. Washington, DC: USCCB, 2005.

The Compendium, which was designed to supplement the teachings of the Catholic Catechism, is especially helpful in providing a broad comprehensive view of the vast scope of CST. It is divided into twelve chapters:

1. God's Plan of Love for Humanity
2. The Church's Mission and Social Doctrine
3. The Human Person and Human Rights
4. Principles of the Church's Social Doctrine
5. The Family: The Vital Cell of Society
6. Human Work
7. Economic Life
8. The Political Community
9. The International Community
10. Safeguarding the Environment
11. The Promotion of Peace
12. Social Doctrine and Ecclesial Action

This volume treats a wide variety of issues: disarmament, terrorism, globalization, biotechnology, foreign debt, the role of the free market, Jesus as a man of work, the tragedy of sin, and creating a civilization of love.

Rowlands, Anna. *Toward a Politics of Communion: Catholic Social Teaching in Dark Times.* London: Bloomsbury Publishing, 2021.

Papal biographer Austen Ivereigh called Rowlands's book "an astonishing achievement" and "the definitive contemporary guide to CST." Rowlands, who teaches theology at Durham University, is an internationally respected scholar who helped draft the working document for the 2023 Synod in Rome and served as a theological consultant during the Synod. Her book places CST in the context of modern political, economic, and social movements. It has chapters on human dignity, subsidiarity, solidarity, and the universal distribution of goods that relate directly to the themes of CST, as well as chapters that illumine the other themes. In all my commentaries on the seven themes I have incorporated material from Rowlands's sophisticated analysis, hopefully bringing her outstanding work to a wider American audience.

SELECTED BIBLIOGRAPHY

Articles and Documents

Acton Staff. "Initial Reactions to *Centesimus Annus*." *Religion and Liberty* 1, no 3 (2010).

Alafriz, Olivia. "'Poisoning the Blood of Our Country': Trump Delivers Caustic Attack on Immigrants." *Politico*, December 16, 2023. www.politico.com/news/2023/12/16/trump-immigration-attack -00132156.

Asher, July. "Archbishop Cordileone Says No Communion for Speaker Pelosi over Position on Abortion." *National Catholic Reporter*, May 20, 2022. www.ncronline.org/news/people/archbishop-cordileone-says-no -communion-speaker-pelosi-over-position-abortion.

"At First, I Thought I Was Fighting to Save Rubber Trees. Now I Realize I Am Fighting for Humanity: The Fortieth Newsletter (2019)." *Tricontinental*, October 3, 2019. thetricontinental.org/newsletterissue/at-first -i-thought-i-was-fighting-to-save-rubber-trees-now-i-realize-i-am -fighting-for-humanity-the-fortieth-newsletter-2019.

Benedict XVI, Pope. "Message of His Holiness Pope Benedict XVI for the Celebration of the World Day of Peace." January 1, 2006. www.vatican .va/content/benedict-xvi/en/messages/peace/documents/hf_ben-xvi _mes_20051213_xxxix-world-day-peace.html.

"Bishop Asks for Prayers for New President and Vice President, Calls for Dialogue and Collaboration." *San Diego Catholic*, January 20, 2021. sdcatholic.org/news-release/bishop-asks-for-prayers-for-new-pre sident-and-vice-president-calls-for-dialogue-and-collaboration.

Bradner, Eric. "Joe Biden Was Denied Communion at Catholic Church in South Carolina." *CNN*, October 29, 2019. www.cnn.com/2019/10/

29/politics/joe-biden-denied-communion-south-carolina-catholic
-church/index.html.

Cavanagh, William T. "No War Is Good: Lamenting—Not Cheer-
leading—the War in Ukraine." *Commonweal*, May 10, 2023. www
.commonwealmagazine.org/ukraine-war-francis-nonviolence-putin
-cavanaugh.

"Chaput Says Denying Biden Communion Is 'Pastoral' Not 'Political.'"
Catholic News Agency, December 4, 2020. www.catholicnewsagency
.com/news/46807/chaput-says-denying-biden-communion-is
-pastoral-not-political.

Committee on Migration. "Following Court Decision on DACA, U.S.
Bishops' Migration Chairman Renews Plea for Congress to Provide
Legislative Solution." USCCB, October 6, 2022. www.usccb.org/news/
2022/following-court-decision-daca-us-bishops-migration-chairman
-renews-plea-congress-provide.

———. "USCCB Committee on Migration Chair Strongly Opposes Executive Order Because It Harms Vulnerable Refugee and Immigrant
Families." USCCB, February 6, 2017. www.usccb.org/news/2017/
usccb-committee-migration-chair-strongly-opposes-executive-order
-because-it-harms.

Day, Dorothy. "Our Country Passes from Undeclared War to Declared
War; We Continue Our Christian Pacifist Stand." *The Catholic Worker*,
January 1, 1942. catholicworker.org/868-html.

DeSanctis, Alexandra. "Garry Wills Is Wrong about the Bishops and
Abortion." *National Review*, June 28, 2021. www.nationalreview.com/
corner/garry-wills-is-wrong-about-the-bishops-and-abortion.

"Editorial: Bishops' Pastoral Letter on Racism Lacks Sustained Urgency."
National Catholic Reporter, November 19, 2018. www.ncronline.org/
opinion/editorial/editorial-bishops-pastoral-letter-racism-lacks
-sustained-urgency.

Flynn, J. D. "The 'Message' of McElroy's Red Hat." *The Pillar*, May 29,
2022. www.pillarcatholic.com/p/the-message-of-mcelroys-red-hat.

Francis, Pope. "Address of the Holy Father on Nuclear Weapons."
November 24, 2019. www.vatican.va/content/francesco/en/speeches/
2019/november/documents/papa-francesco_20191124_messaggio
-arminucleari-nagasaki.html.

———. "Address of the Holy Father: Visit to the Joint Session of the United States Congress." September 24, 2015. www.vatican.va/content/francesco/en/speeches/2015/september/documents/papa-francesco_20150924_usa-us-congress.html.

———. "General Audience." February 9, 2022. www.vatican.va/content/francesco/en/audiences/2022/documents/20220209-udienza-generale.html.

———. "Homily of His Holiness Pope Francis." February 17, 2016. www.vatican.va/content/francesco/en/homilies/2016/documents/papa-francesco_20160217_omelia-messico-ciudad-jaurez.html.

———. "Message of the Holy Father Francis for the Celebration of the World Day of Prayer for the Care of Creation." July 21, 2022. press.vatican.va/content/salastampa/en/bollettino/pubblico/2022/07/21/220721c.html.

———. "Video Message of the Holy Father on the Occasion of the Launch of the Laudato si' Action Platform." May 25, 2021. press.vatican.va/content/salastampa/en/bollettino/pubblico/2021/05/25/210525c.html.

General Motors News Release Details. "General Motors, the Largest U.S. Automaker, Plans to Be Carbon Neutral by 2040." GM.com, January 28, 2021. investor.gm.com/news-releases/news-release-details/general-motors-largest-us-automaker-plans-be-carbon-neutral-2040.

Gomez, José Horacio. "USCCB President's Statement on the Inauguration of Joseph R. Biden, Jr., as 46th President of the United States of America." USCCB, January 20, 2021. www.usccb.org/news/2021/usccb-presidents-statement-inauguration-joseph-r-biden-jr-46th-president-united-states.

Gordon, Mary. "This Pregnancy: Each One Is Different." *Commonweal*, November 1, 2022. www.commonwealmagazine.org/pregnancy.

Horan, Daniel P. "The Bishops' Letter Fails to Recognize That Racism Is a White Problem." *National Catholic Reporter*, February 20, 2019. www.ncronline.org/opinion/faith-seeking-understanding/bishops-letter-fails-recognize-racism-white-problem.

John Paul II, Pope. "Address to the Diplomatic Corps, January 16, 1993." *Origins* 22, no. 34 (February 4, 1993).

———. "Address to the International Conference on Nutrition." *Origins* 22, no. 28 (December 24, 1992).

Kaveny, Cathleen. "Who Trusts the Pro-Life Movement? Abortion and a Child Rape Victim in Ohio." *Commonweal*, November 27, 2022. www.commonwealmagazine.org/abortion-ohio-kaveny-women-GOP-rape.

Mayaki, Benedict. "Pope: Volunteers Are the Strength of the Church." *Vatican News*, December 5, 2022. www.vaticannews.va/en/pope/news/2022-12/pope-francis-volunteers-volunteering-world-day-video-message.html.

Migration and Refugee Services/Office of Migration Policy and Public Affairs. "Catholic Church's Position on Immigration Reform." USCCB, August 2013.

O'Kane, Lydia. "Pope Francis: Care for Water Is Urgent Imperative." *Vatican News*, September 1, 2018. www.vaticannews.va/en/pope/news/2018-09/pope-francis-care-for-water-is-urgent-imperative.html.

Pattison, Mark. "Bishop Warns against 'Weaponization of Eucharist' with Elected Officials." *National Catholic Reporter*, February 2, 2021. www.ncronline.org/news/bishop-warns-against-weaponization-eucharist-elected-officials.

Republic Title. "History of Earth Day." April 22, 2024. www.republictitle.com/earth-day.

Rocca, Francis X. "Catholic Bishops Debate Communion for Biden, Politicians Who Support Abortion Rights." *Wall Street Journal*, June 17, 2021. www.wsj.com/articles/catholic-bishops-debate-communion-for-biden-11623937299.

Seitz, Mark. "Bishop Seitz on Biden's New Asylum Policy: Death Cannot Be the Cost of Our Immigration Laws." *America*, March 14, 2023. www.americamagazine.org/politics-society/2023/03/14/biden-asylum-immigration-244876.

Trump, Donald. "Donald Trump 2016 RNC Draft Speech Transcript." *Politico*, July 21, 2016. www.politico.com/story/2016/07/full-transcript-donald-trump-nomination-acceptance-speech-at-rnc-225974.

United Nations Climate Change. "What Is the Triple Planetary Crisis?" UNCC, April 13, 2022. unfccc.int/news/what-is-the-triple-planetary-crisis.

USCCB. "USCCB Statement on U.S. Supreme Court Ruling in *Dobbs v. Jackson*." June 24, 2022. www.usccb.org/news/2022/usccb-statement-us-supreme-court-ruling-dobbs-v-jackson.

Wester, John C. "Living in the Light of Christ's Peace: A Conversation toward Nuclear Disarmament." January 11, 2022. files.ecatholic.com/17613/documents/2022/1/220111_ABW_Pastoral_Letter_LivingintheLightofChristsPeace_Official_Reduced.pdf?t=1641922875000.

Wilkinson, Tracy. "Pope Francis Is a Biden fan, but Some U.S. Catholic Leaders Give President a Frosty Reception." *Los Angeles Times*, February 3, 2021. www.latimes.com/politics/story/2021-02-03/u-s-catholic-group-giving-biden-a-surprisingly-frosty-reception.

Wills, Garry. "The Bishops Are Wrong about Biden—and Abortion." *New York Times*, June 27, 2021. www.nytimes.com/2021/06/27/opinion/biden-bishops-communion-abortion.html.

Winright, Tobias. "The Possibility of a Just War." *Commonweal*, May 2023. www.commonwealmagazine.org/possibility-just-war.

Winters, Michael Sean. "2022 Saw Opposition to Pope Francis, Plus Intellectual and Ecclesial Shifts." *National Catholic Reporter*, December 26, 2022. www.ncronline.org/opinion/ncr-voices/2022-saw-opposition-pope-francis-plus-intellectual-and-ecclesial-shifts.

Books

Cahill, Lisa Sowle. *Blessed Are the Peacemakers: Pacifism, Just War, and Peacebuilding*. Minneapolis: Fortress Press, 2019.

Chenoweth, Erica, and Maria J. Stephan. *Why Civil Resistance Works: The Strategic Logic of Nonviolent Conflict*. New York: Columbia University Press, 2012.

Curran, Charles. *Catholic Social Teaching: A Historical, Theological and Ethical Analysis*. Washington, DC: Georgetown University Press, 2002.

CATHOLIC SOCIAL TEACHING

Gilligan, Carol. *In a Different Voice: Psychological Theory and Women's Development*. Cambridge, MA: Harvard University Press, 2016.

Himes, Kenneth R., ed. *Modern Catholic Social Teaching: Commentaries and Interpretations*. Washington, DC: Georgetown University Press, 2005.

Mich, Marvin Krier. *Catholic Social Teaching and Movements*. Mystic, CT: Twenty-Third Publications, 1994.

www.ingramcontent.com/pod-product-compliance
Ingram Content Group UK Ltd.
Pitfield, Milton Keynes, MK11 3LW, UK
UKHW022126090925
462749UK00004B/54